Field Guide to Indoor Urbanism

Acknowledgments

The *Field Guide to Indoor Urbanism* has been made possible by the support of the Knowlton School of the Ohio State University, the RISD Professional Development Fund, and the New York State Council on the Arts with the support of the Office of the Governor and the New York State Legislature. For their contributions to the book, we would like to thank graphic designer Sarah Gephart of MGMT. design, and editors Zoë Slutzky and James Graham. We would also like to thank architects Fumihiko Maki, Itsuko Hasegawa, Kengo Kuma, Ryue Nishizawa, Takaharu with Yui Tezuka, and Go Hasegawa for our conversations in Tokyo about architecture and the environment.

MODU works in multiple modes of practice—client projects, urban interventions, proactive initiatives, and socio-environmental research. It would not be possible to work concurrently within these modes without numerous instrumental team members. We would like to thank Tom Sterling, Diego Fernandez Morales, Kamilla Csegzi, Jiri Vala, Amanda Morgan, and Ammr Vandal. We also thank all of MODU's current and past team members for their contributions.

MODU's projects involve numerous collaborations with experts from other disciplines. Some of these interdisciplinary collaborations span across projects for years. We would like to thank landscape architect Kristi Cheramie, climate engineer Erik Olsen of Transsolar, historian David Serlin, structural engineer Scott Hughes of Silman, and music composer Jonathan Berger.

Over meetings and dinner tables, conversations with friends and colleagues have influenced and shaped our work. Some conversations evolved into this book; in particular, we would like to thank Enrique Walker, Dominic Leong, and Marc Tsurumaki. We would also like to thank others with whom we've been in conversation for years: Bernard Tschumi, Keller Easterling, William Feuerman, Matan Sapir, François Nguyen, Mimi Hoang, Eric Bunge, Roy Rotem, Deanna Van Buren, Juan Herreros, Leslie Gill, Richard Gluckman, Hussein Fancy, Adam Frampton, Emanuel Admassu, Raquel Ramati, Elaine Molinar, Theresa Genovese, Paul Lewis, Dan Handel, Simon Goode, and Matias Honorato.

Fellowships have been invaluable platforms, providing time and space for asking essential questions. We are deeply grateful to the American Academy of Rome for the Rome Prize and the National Endowment for the Arts for the US–Japan Creative Artist fellowship. Key projects in the book were made possible by the generous support of organizations including The Ripple Foundation and the Rauschenberg Foundation.

Contents

Projects

Second Nature

Forward:
Indoor Urbanism

Glossary

Lexicon Terms

The glossary is the outcome of a cross-disciplinary process of generating design concepts and strategies. Each term is seemingly a contradiction; together, they argue for architecture and the environment as extensions of each another. The terms engage cultural diversity; each term can be read from left to right or right to left—encouraging new meanings from reinterpretations.

Air Corridor

In an abandoned hotel in Sicily, a woman abruptly stops as she witnesses an anxious black bird banging on narrow corridor walls to escape. An air corridor is an enabler of random encounters, a path of thermal relief as breezes move through. It allows for energy flow at multiple scales, from hallways in houses to corridors in buildings and avenues in cities.

Bird Companion

A northern cardinal, an annual visitor in spring, performs a flying lesson to a fledgling in the back yard—a cross-species relationship that neither one is dependent on the other. Establish a provisional trust while occupying shared space and time. The fragile assurance of normalcy is through repetitive encounters.

Button Soup

An old parable about how to make a rich, flavored soup with very limited ingredients. Ideas are always tested and developed at different economies of scale. An additive process is induced with patience and optimism.

Cat Logic

On a cold winter day in Rome, a cat sanctuary within a hospital courtyard is empty. Cats are found hovering above the hospital's warm mechanical vents. Though humanized to speak as in a Haruki Murakami novel, thermal comfort informs their preferences rather than social connectivity.

Circular Time

Establish an ecology of culture through cross-generational dialogue. Inclusiveness built through a return to questions of the beginning. The ordinary never settles as it is always renewed. The return to the naivety of youth as a generator of continuous change.

Collective Weather

The beginning of a conversation made with a familiar stranger. A universal notion that is personally experienced yet socially exchanged. Environmental resilience formed through the shared awareness of climate change.

Crafted Nature Botanical gardens in Tokyo are attentively cared for yet seem untouched. Hundreds of years of nature cultivation by humans reach an aesthetic sublime. As climate becomes more extreme, fragile ecosystems will become more dependent on human interventions.

Digital Weather Weather control achieved in nonstop interiors that muted the unpredictability of the outdoors. Passive data of connectivity dissipate in flatland. The uniformity of sensorial environment builds up an indoor atmosphere of restlessness. A technological glitch is as exciting as a passing breeze.

Dual Futures A parking deck as a speculation for an open future. Design for both, transforming from one to another. In our societies of continual change, an intended program is often outlasted by the building itself. Raising questions about how we define architectural completion.

Extinct Sounds What is your favorite extinct animal? A composer revives lost sounds through digital simulations, mimicking the path of air going through ancient lungs. Sounds that provoke sadness of lost ancient memories. Emphasize the fragility of the environment while amplifying the removed.

Familiar Stranger A familiar face crosses one's path in day-to-day rituals. Unclear if a social gesture of greeting is appropriate, eyes blink to remember any past interaction. An awkward moment of non-engagement signals that this is just another day. A sense of belonging to a place is achieved by inclusion of the recognizable.

Flexible Gaps A path for breezes to flush a sweltering city in between buildings in Tokyo. A movement of wood joints in response to weather change allow for flexible structures. Separators between one to another. Small scale relative to its surrounding. Provide possibilities for alternate futures as elements are kept independent of each other.

Futurist Moment Living between two different time scales. Connect the future to the passing moment. Present belongs to the instinctive, clipped perspective. The future to the intentional, distant aerial view. Explore the logical future with the sentiment of the moment.

Glossary

Hearing Plants   Nectar production by plants is enhanced with the buzzing sounds of approaching bees. Acknowledging attributes of hearing to the silenced forms of the living can foster empathy. Living through shared experiences between species.

Human Bee   Dancing is not exclusive to humans. A behavior of the many is shared between species. Connectivity is scaleless as we are part of one ecology. The disappearance of one species will impact on the future of another.

Incomplete Whole   Architecture itself is always incomplete, embodying many potential scenarios and no fixed outcomes. While it cannot be completed, perhaps it can be made whole in connecting people with the environment.

Indoor Rain   A contemporary Roman fountain in an incomplete Italian ruin. Rain finds its way through holes of unfinished floor slabs of never used electric outlets. Exposed interiors open to seasonality and weathering provides shelter to dogs and nesting birds.

Invisible Blue   Culturally not yet defined, the blue in the sky had no name in early times. The blue planet was not detected from a perspective of being within. Only to be named later, it became a concept in the background of the yellow dunes of Egypt, blue evolved into a longing.

Limitless Interiors   Accelerated by global epidemics. Virtual spaces enabled by technology have replaced physical spaces, connections made through working, learning, and socializing. The more we find ourselves in here, the more we feel the need for daily direct connection with the outdoors.

Map Holes   A world map that does not presume to be complete. Unfinished maps acknowledge not knowing. An order that is not whole. A map of open questions. Understand that data alone is never complete or finalized.

Mechanical Delirium   Promised a summer break visit at the museum. Enter through the back freight elevator, stop at the mechanical floor. Put oversized soundproof headphones on. Large chillers buzz, pipe pathways checked. Sensors' data are looked at, head back. Exhibit still awaits.

Memoryless Ruin	Hundreds of construction beginnings never completed in Sicily. Perpetually in a state of the temporary. Decay before ever reaching its prime. Memories were not formed or collected. Awaits futures with alternative histories.
Momentary Library	Library of open books, flipping pages is between a group of books rather than a single one. Spatially organized, carefully marked and read multiple times. Knowledge is learned in linking multiple points of views.
Nondescript Architecture	A music venue is held under a highway in New Orleans protesting the loss of a space of culture. An architecture of momentary social action as the enabler of the intermittent in-between indoors and outdoors. An environment that permits activism.
Occasional Architecture	Rave parties held in highway underpasses and DJ booths hidden in underground shelters. The birthplace of the LGBTQ movement in Tel Aviv. Originally designed as infrastructure, their invaluable significance is to provide a space in times of hardship for the marginalized.
Outdoor Interiors	A movie is playing in a piazza in Rome. Programs of indoors migrate outdoors. A momentary intimacy shared with strangers. The urban accepts the gentleness of indoor behaviors as the young help elders with stacking their chairs at the end.
Public Floor	The horizontal city that is otherwise defined by its verticality. Chaotic, crowded, and noisy, it is open to misinterpretations and redefinition of normal. It is in public spaces like this where we experience the freedom to be ourselves among others that are different than us.
Quiet Noise	Sounds of nature are more pronounced as machines are silenced. The blue color of the sky is more vivid as air pollution recedes. Through temporary disappearance, the human impact on Earth has never been more noticeable.
Season House	Migrate through microclimates and topographies within the lines of a lot in the ancient Roman domus. Warm kitchen turns into a living room. Breezy roof into a bedroom. House that is not defined by room types but by microclimates of comfort.

Glossary

Second Nature
Lower the voice when entering a bare concrete library in Tokyo. Nuanced social behavior that is associated with a place. Architecture as a dual expression of social and environmental contexts. Humans and nature as one.

Sense Making
Loss of social touch in times of distancing. Sense deprivation influences our environments in new ways that would provide us with alternative means of communication. Sensory enhancement of other senses is an opportunity to design new experiences.

Small Vastness
A small room within an empty urban square in Beijing. Simultaneously consider both extra small and extremely large. Both impact each other as the interior coarsens and the urban softens. Rethinking the boundaries between outdoors and indoors, bringing together unexpected events.

Social Particle
Riding a motorbike alongside millions of others that flood the streets of Saigon. Space that allows for a flow of many people to behave as one. Change momentarily the perception of self. Feeling afloat while surrendering to the crowd.

Social Weathers
A museum in Hakone offers hot springs to revitalize tired feet after wandering around. Where strangers meet for a shared moment of contradiction. Neither indoors nor outdoors. A place of social pause between public and private expectations.

Temporary Humans
In a museum on Teshima Island, a room for humans during the day and animals at night. Acknowledgment of the temporary state of being human and the long existence of architecture on the planet. It is a design for ruination at multiple scales of inhabiting earth.

Together Alone
A group of young adults physically congregate together while interacting digitally. Sitting informally, a social state of fragmented intimacy between physical nearness and social remoteness. Social relationship of the instant leaves one incomplete.

Tree Culture
A museum where nature is both the platform and the content. Expand the definition of cultural production to all living things. Design a cultural space for trees to communicate and for nonhumans to socialize within the urban context.

Urban Fields	Reintroduce fields of nature into cities. Past childhood memories reconnect to the urban grid. Vacant neighborhoods become green with rural nature. Provide small freedoms during times of oversurveillance. Happily, lost in the midst.
Weather Drawing	Drawing the ephemeral qualities of the invisible. Where borders are not defined by walls but by the laws of thermodynamics. Space, not as a static design, but a constant change of performance. Synthesis of weather and architecture.
Weather Memory	Driving through the Negev desert in the overheated summer. Get winter coats from the back of the car. Pass through one door after another. Eyes adjust to the vast cave-like space. The cold air hurts. A massive, refrigerated room containing packaged dates are ready for shipment overseas.
Weather Room	Close viewing of snowfall while being mostly sheltered. The room is both urban and interior, with its environmental experiences. It is partially open to the exterior, created by the subtraction of architectural elements.
White Dust	Measured on the rooftops of Manhattan rather than on its ground floor. Sectional misreading of its social and environmental impact. Camouflaged particles that turn the atmosphere into an interior condition of separation.
Wild Urbanism	Temporarily abandoned urban environments are new territories of uncontrolled nature. Rapid moss growth in Piazza Navona after heavy rain. Wild animals roam the alleys in daytime. Beauty of gentle life that manifests itself post-human occupancy.
Yellow Time	A title of a book that was never returned to a library. The beginning of winter is marked by the yellow blossoms of Asteroideae flowers in the Middle East. The dust from their seeds seeks new territory. A drifting landscape that keeps moving north in space and back in time with the migrating climate.

Rachely Rotem with Phu Hoang

Public Floor

Mapping: Horizontal City
Episode: Invisible Atmopheres
Public Floor: Walking Through New York

Mapping:
Horizontal City

Financial District, Manhattan
Along the East River's waterfront, outdoor yoga classes are held during the summer. The grass is covered by yoga mats. Classes may be canceled to accommodate for the unpredictability of the weather. Their location alternates between the open lawn and the comfort of shaded trees, which is also dependent on the forecast. They become popular during the COVID-19 pandemic since indoor gyms are closed and online classes can be solitary experiences. Rethinking previously held indoor activities has turned them into opportunities for mindful engagement with the outdoors.

Legend

Building Shade (Winter & Summer)

Tree Shade (Winter & Summer)

Sidewalk

Public Park

Outdoor Dining (Winter & Summer)

Bus Shelter (Winter & Summer)

Open Streets (COVID-19)

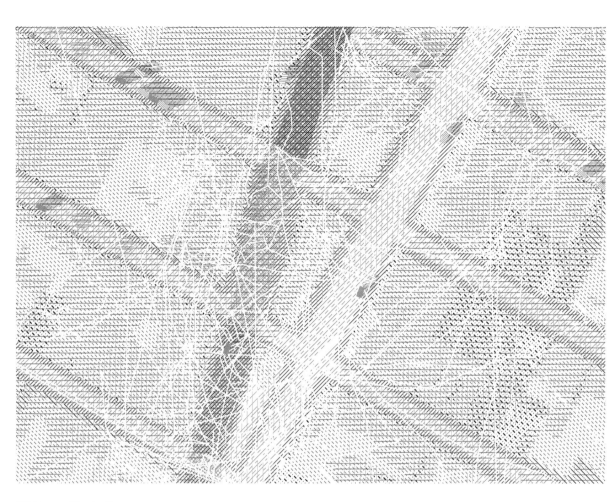

Midtown, Manhattan

It is wintertime in New York and a street performer, the Naked Cowboy, is doing his act in the city's most recognizable public space: Times Square. He is one of many who perform outdoors in all seasons, changing costumes in the bathrooms of nearby coffee chains. Their income depends on daily foot traffic, working for tips in exchange for photos. The Naked Cowboy has been there for over twenty-three years, dressed only in underpants, boots, and a cowboy hat. He continues to perform, even as Times Square empties out during cold weather. His resilience to the weather has itself become the performance.

Nolita, Manhattan

The owner of an antique store gets approval from municipal authorities for the interim use of a city-owned empty lot. Over many years, he plants a garden and places antiques inside for the exclusive use of his store. The public could experience it from behind a fence or reach it through the store, which has direct access to the lot. One day, when the city announced plans to develop the lot for affordable senior housing, the owner creates a nonprofit organization, opens Elizabeth Gardens to the public, and advocates for its use as a public space. Though the garden has become an oasis for neighborhood residents and visitors, its future will be determined in court, as both green spaces and affordable housing are in scarce supply.

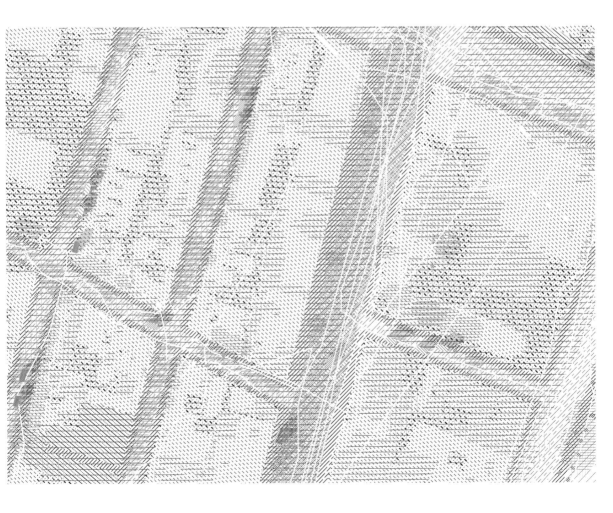

Carroll Gardens, Brooklyn
During the COVID-19 pandemic, commercial streets become sites of community activation, creatively extending a lifeline to small businesses during challenging times. A pub restaurant turns its side yard, typically used for dining in most seasons, into a children's skating rink during the winter. A French restaurant sets up a ping-pong table on the sidewalk and hosts spontaneous tournaments among those waiting for a takeout order. This game table remains outside when the restaurant is closed, used during the night by its neighbors.

Above: Thermal-image drawing; sidewalk ping-pong table invites impromptu matches outside a local restaurant

Brooklyn Heights
A performance by a neighborhood theater group takes place in the early days of summer. Partially on the street's sidewalk and partially inside an empty storefront, the group of singers move between the threshold of private and public, indoors and outdoors. They sing to the seated audience as well as to those passing by, performing a baroque-style opera while singing the words of the US Constitution. Just as the translation of historic text into lyrics brings new perspectives to the Constitution, the indoor/outdoor theater opens the experience of performance into one of the city's largest public spaces— the sidewalk.

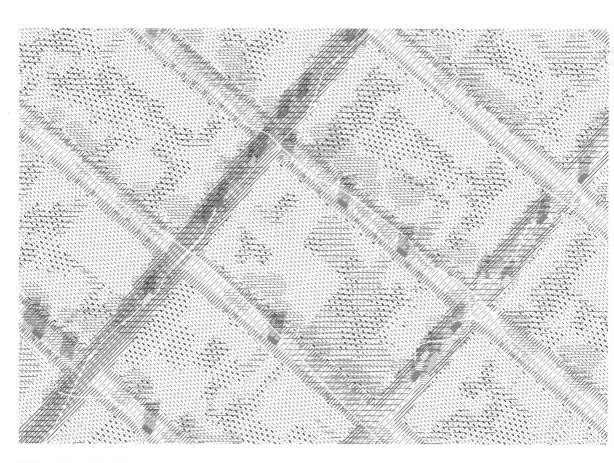

Williamsburg, Brooklyn

The city permits restaurants and bars to use their adjacent sidewalks and parking lanes to construct outdoor sheds. The temporary use of these sheds for outdoor dining becomes a citywide reality, extending interior activities to the outdoors. This extension of the seasonal use of the outdoors employs commonplace materials and products—corrugated metal roofs, acrylic wall panels, heat lamps. Diners keep their coats on for an extra layer of warmth, with some restaurants offering blankets for colder weather. The rudimentary nature of the sheds' construction is countered with the warmth of amenities like heat lamps. This new custom brings people together by allowing them to choose socializing safely over the comfort of the indoors.

Above: New York's Open Restaurant program results in outdoor dining sheds, with heat lamps for all-weather dining

Eastchester Gardens, Bronx
A superblock that is owned by the New York City Housing Authority faces challenges from privatization. In its early days, before the installation of air conditioning, the open space between the buildings used to be a cool green space for family-oriented activities during the hot summer months. Today, most residents keep their children indoors. NYCHA contemplates selling the underutilized land that it owns in between the buildings to private developers. As the need to access outdoor spaces becomes more evident, some advocate for keeping the outdoor spaces for current residents and prioritizing investments, thus making them safer and more approachable for the residents' well-being. Others advocate using new funding from private development to develop more affordable public housing elsewhere.

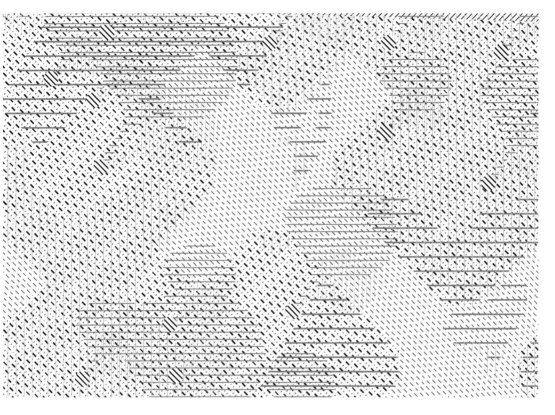

Left: Thermal-image drawing;
underutilized open spaces of Eastchester
Gardens public housing projects

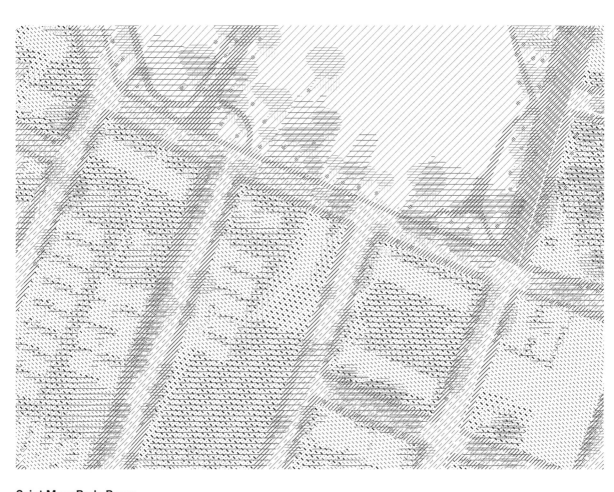

Saint Mary Park, Bronx
As an anchor park in the Bronx, it is the site of New York's first indoor recreation center. Its location in the park allows for public programs that are both indoors and outdoors. The center has a temporary outdoor library, and art stations for children are periodically set up. Tents for shade and bookshelves with wheels are provided to negotiate the unpredictability of the weather. Unlike in an interior library, reading out loud is encouraged and provides the comfort level of an informal engagement in urban nature.

Flushing, Queens
Roosevelt Avenue's sidewalks are shaded
by the elevated subway train above and are
loud, chaotic, and bustling with urban life.
Queens is one of the most diverse areas in
the world, with hundreds of international
restaurants representing over twenty-
five food cultures. It is a community of
small business owners that showcase the
community's resilience during economically
challenging times. The proximity of
ethnicities occurs within the public sphere,
but not among the diners. Each culture
stays within the familiar boundaries of
culinary experiences.

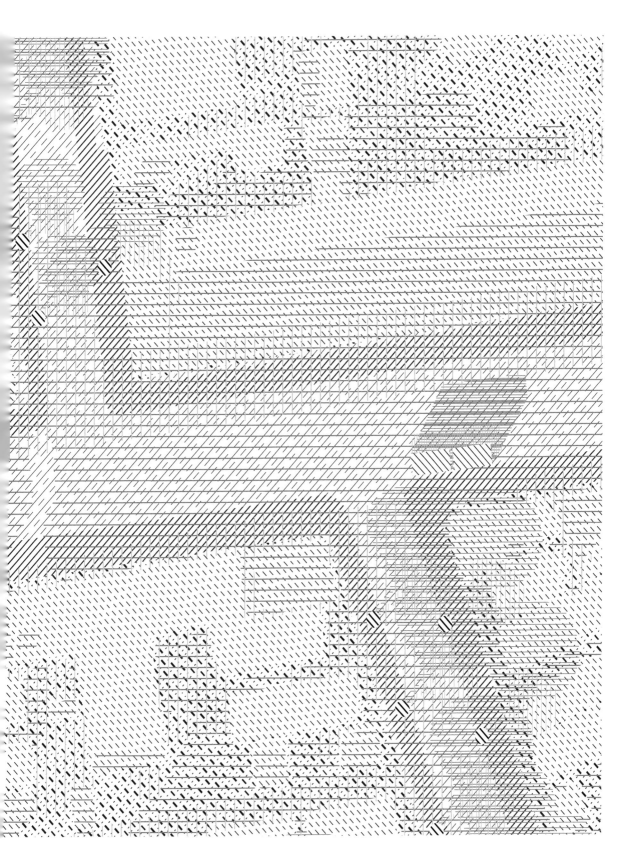

Episode:
Invisible Atmospheres

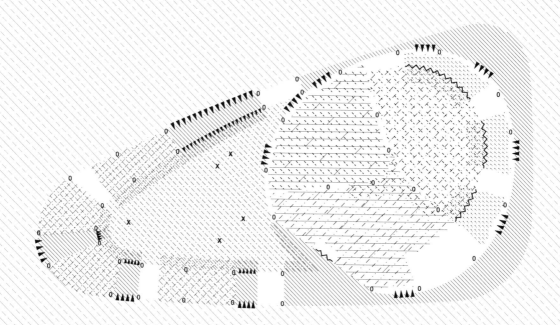

Invisible Atmospheres are **weather drawings** exploring the idea that the environment modifies architecture, rather than architecture's separation from the environment. Completed for various projects—from architecture to cultural installations to urban imaginaries—they are tools to render visible invisible atmospheres like temperature, humidity, or even static electricity. The multiplication of lines questions resolute borders between architecture and the environment; overlapping "fronts" of lines create densities that signal thresholds and transitions.

Above: Abstract dust drawing of airborne silica particle for Weather Uncontrol installation

Opposite: Microclimate plan for the Playgarden kindergarten proposal

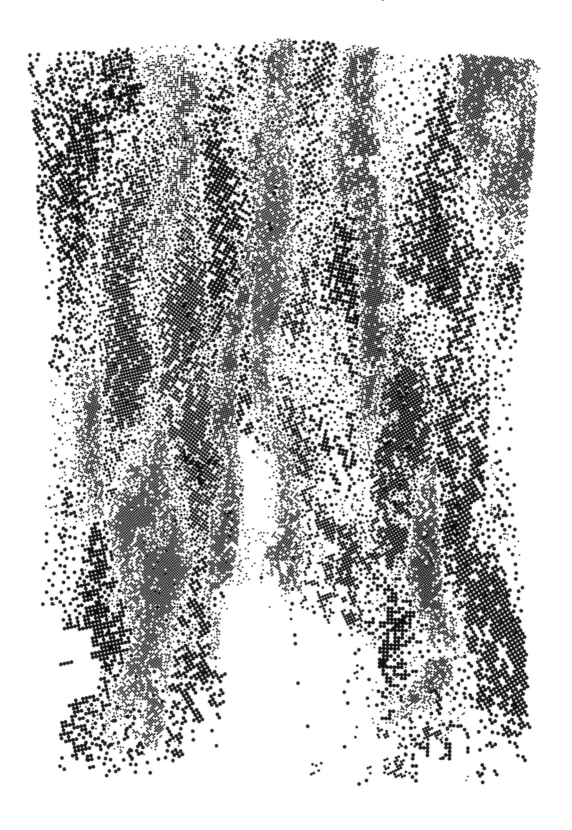

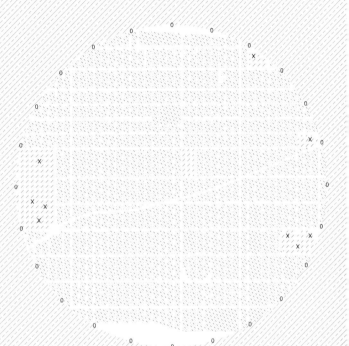

Above: Living Outside the Dome; climate plan of Buckminster Fuller's Dome over Manhattan

Opposite: One of many shade scenarios from suspended balls on the ceiling of the Cloud Seeding pavilion

Public Floor: Walking through New York

Phu Hoang with Rachely Rotem

Public Shade Sidewalks

Manhattan has long been defined by its physical borders, which have determined its growth. Within these limits, New York City has developed its vertical identity, multiplying height by density. This vertical city is also a city of walls, inscribing environmental and social borders through separation. On one side of the walls, it is private and indoors; the other side is public and outdoors. Yet between the walls of this vertical city there remains a less-theorized space even more crucial to the everyday lives of its residents.

Understanding the urban sidewalk as a "public floor" shifts emphasis away from the vertical character of New York City's boroughs to foreground the **horizontal city**. Chaotic, crowded, and noisy, the experiences of the public floor occur across walls, characterized by the daily and seasonal changes of its interconnected ground. This is not just a city of transactions, but interactions. The public floor is inhabited by book vendors on sidewalks, construction workers resting under trees, and doormen opening lobby doors. It is composed of the sidewalks, restaurants, streets, shops, and parks that are interior and urban, private and public, open and closed.

New York's sidewalks, over 12,000 miles long and one of its largest public spaces, have an essential role in interconnecting the public floor.[1] Sidewalks link ground-floor interiors with urban infrastructure and open-air exteriors with conditioned atmospheres. They also register changing environmental conditions, especially the seasonal shade cast by trees, buildings, and small urban infrastructure (bus stops, newsstands, kiosks). Mapping these sidewalks documents the ephemeral character of urban public shade and its opportunities for social connectivity. Its microclimates, especially the tree canopy, have an important role in reducing urban heat islands.

Tree Culture

New York's **tree culture**, whether in public rights-of-way, city parks, or forested natural areas, cover 22 percent of the city's public floor.[2] Its environmental role includes cooling streets and buildings, removing carbon, facilitating air filtration, and increasing biodiversity. Its social benefits combine better health and well-being while strengthening communities. These environmental and social aspects have become increasingly relevant with the climate crisis, as the climate zone of the New York region has changed from humid continental to humid subtropical.[3] This migrating climate has brought higher humidity and increased heat waves—in frequency, intensity, and duration.

Above top: Plant store in Chinatown extending retail interiors onto sidewalk

Above bottom: More indoor activities can occur outdoors with varied microclimates

However, trees and their shade are not distributed equally in New York. The neighborhoods with the least trees, such as Mott Haven in the Bronx, have the highest heat vulnerability index. In these predominantly minority neighborhoods, urban heat islands reveal inequities of outdoor comfort; higher income neighborhoods have cooler microclimates, with surface temperatures at times thirty degrees lower than in lower-income areas.[4] This follows the city's other environmental inequalities, especially air quality and health. Urban shade is recognized in all its forms, for both natural and built environments. While planting more trees is essential, shade and ventilation include architecture: public shade structures, open-air interiors, and buildings designed for natural ventilation. In addition to planting trees along the sidewalk and street edge, trees can also be integrated with building exteriors to increase shade. Both increased access and diverse forms of shade would produce thermal diversity in more neighborhoods while making New York more climate adaptable.

Public Floor Design

Given the climate crisis, architects and designers have a role in improving quality and access to outdoor comfort while mitigating the impact of urban heat islands. Expanding the threshold between indoors and outdoors is an important way to achieve this, as the modernist dilemma of fully conditioned interiors has proven to be an unhealthy regime. The public floor offers opportunities with microclimate spaces—a form of **second nature**—in between interior and urban environments. A wide range of public shade and natural ventilation creates healthy environments that mitigate heat risk and vulnerability. This is the essential argument of the public floor, and it is, at its essence, a design issue.

One asks the architectural and environmental questions that relate to design. Reexamining the borders between indoor and outdoor environments prompts: What is a sidewalk, a restaurant, a street, or a shop? What, even, does it mean to walk through a city now? Reshaping the public realm with wider sidewalks and more parks and plazas, as well as interior environments with fresh air ventilation and equitable access to outdoor spaces, demonstrates the importance of an active and accessible public floor.

Pandemic Epilogue

In the spring of 2020, the global COVID-19 pandemic transformed New York and its public floor. To counter **limitless interiors**, sidewalks and their shade became an essential part of a public health campaign to increase access to the outdoors. Being outside was proven to lower the risk of virus transmission, and expansive areas of public shade

improved outdoor comfort. New York, more than other US cities, was the site of a massive social experiment reconceiving long-held environmental borders. Activities that commonly occurred indoors were extended to the outdoors, which prompted new conceptions of both environments.

Above top: Streets closed for Black Lives Matter rally in New York

Above bottom: New York's Open Streets program; a neighborhood street closed for children to play

These changes to the city's public floor were enacted with administrative policy. In April 2020, Mayor Bill de Blasio announced that 100 miles of city streets would be closed to vehicular traffic through the Open Streets program.[5] In the first six weeks of the Open Restaurants program, 6,700 permits were provided for outdoor dining on city sidewalks and parking lanes. In addition, twenty-two streets were closed for additional outdoor dining.[6] The Open Storefronts program extended commercial activities onto sidewalks, including restaurant takeout operations. These programs made more diffuse the border between interiors and exteriors. The walls that had defined much of New York seemed to disappear—suddenly, everything seemed to be happening in the open air. Daily experiences involved occupying in-between thresholds not simply as pass-through spaces, but places to locate indoor-outdoor activities.

As New York's open-city programs continued over the period of the pandemic, it became apparent that the existing inequities of public shade extended to its temporary forms. Outdoor dining structures provided shade for diners. When outfitted with heaters and fans, they were warmer microclimates in winter and cooler ones in summer. However, underprivileged neighborhoods with their minority communities had fewer permits filed for outdoor restaurants. On average, Manhattan had nearly four times as many outdoor restaurants permits per 100,000 residents than Queens. Comparing individual neighborhoods shows even more disparity: Jamaica, Queens, has twenty-six permits per every 100,000 residents while Tribeca, Manhattan, has over 500. Privatizing the sidewalk by extending outdoor dining also made it less accessible to disadvantaged communities, especially the elderly and people with disabilities.

Over the two-year period of the open-city programs, the benefits of these pandemic protocols have been uneven for both businesses and residents. Rather than improving existing inequities, the programs have only served to amplify them. Like the tree shade on New York's sidewalks, providing better and more access to urban microclimates is the central argument of the public floor.

1. New York City has over 12,000 miles of sidewalks. Retrieved from *NYC.gov*, https://www1.nyc.gov/html/dot/html/infrastructure/sidewalkintro.shtml.

2. "NYC Urban Forest Agenda," The Nature Conservancy, 2021, https://forestforall.nyc/wp-content/uploads/2021/06/NYC-Urban-Forest-Agenda-.pdf.

3. Lisa M. Collins, "Sultry Nights and Magnolia Trees: New York City is Now Subtropical," *The New York Times*, July 24, 2020.

4. John Leland, "Why an East Harlem Street Is 31 Degrees Hotter Than Central Park West," *The New York Times*, August 20, 2021.

5. Ben Yakas, "In Reversal, De Blasio Announces Plan to Open Up To 100 Miles Of Streets To Pedestrians & Cyclists," *Gothamist.com*, April 27, 2020, https://gothamist.com/news/reversal-de-blasio-announces-plan-open-100-miles-streets-pedestrians-cyclists.

6. Pete Wells, "As Dining Takes to the Streets, New York Restaurants Hit a Speed Bump," *The New York Times*, July 2, 2020.

Left: Thermal-image drawing; outdoor yoga class during COVID-19 in Bryant Park, Manhattan

Right: Thermal-image drawing; sidewalk vendors in shade under subway overpass in Flushing, Queens

Projects

Cloud Seeding

Holon, Israel

Mediterranean Climate

MODU with Geotectura

Cloud Seeding is a plaza pavilion, built for Design Museum Holon near Tel Aviv. It is a minimal structure that serves multiple public functions. Below the roof, museum visitors and members of the public can come together to participate in outdoor dance classes, read books on loan from the Mediatheque library, or rest in the shade. The pavilion transforms the overheated and underutilized plaza into an interactive public space, providing access to urban shade.

The pavilion's open-air aluminum frame supports a fabric-mesh ceiling, which allows breezes to circulate, daylight to penetrate, and rain to pass through. Overhead, 30,000 "seeds"—translucent shade balls—move freely. Driven by the wind, the lightweight balls are in continual motion, casting shifting shadows on the ground below. Transparent perforated side panels keep the balls contained within the mesh ceiling while allowing wind to pass through. Lightweight mobile furniture, such as bookshelf carts for a **momentary library**, invites the public to move with the changing shade.

Left: Plaza pavilion mobilizes wind to create a dynamic public space

Opposite: 30,000 balls move with the wind and change the shade on the plaza below

The microclimates of Cloud Seeding are constantly being reconfigured by the interplay of wind and shade. The wind across the plaza becomes an integral part of the architecture, rendered in real time by the moving ceiling. The pavilion brings together two familiar aspects of Israel's built and natural environments, the gabled frame of industrial greenhouses and the Mediterranean Sea breeze, joining them in an experience that is both physical and sensorial. Design Museum Holon's overlooked urban plaza is activated; never the same experience twice, the pavilion's **social weather** combines public urban shade with environmental performance.

Left: Microclimates of shade based on movements of sun and wind

Right: Floor plan; mobile furniture allows for diverse cultural programming

Below: Scenario floor plans; pavilion as outdoor library and house

Next: Daily changes in wind direction and speed define areas of sun and shade

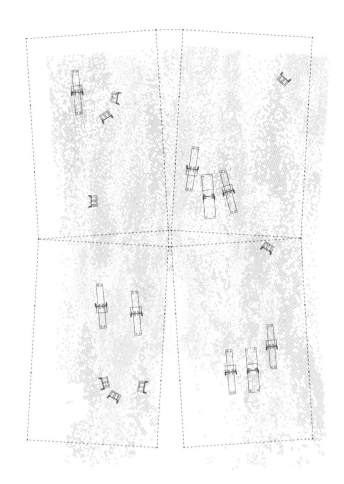

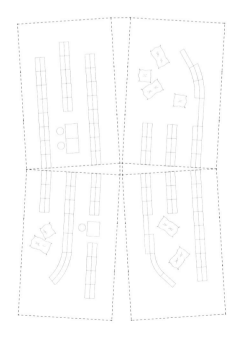

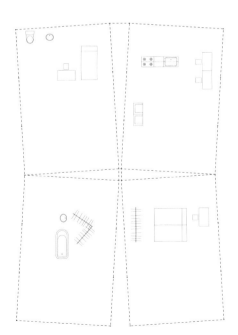

Cloud Seeding

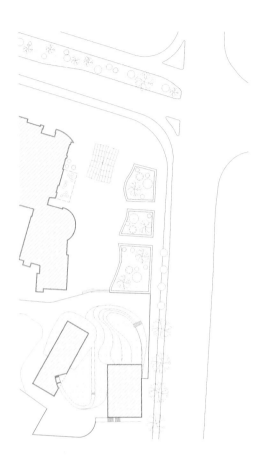

Above: Site plan; the pavilion is in a plaza shared by a design museum and a Mediatheque

Left: The pavilion was designed to be modular for future use in other plazas in the city

Cloud Seeding

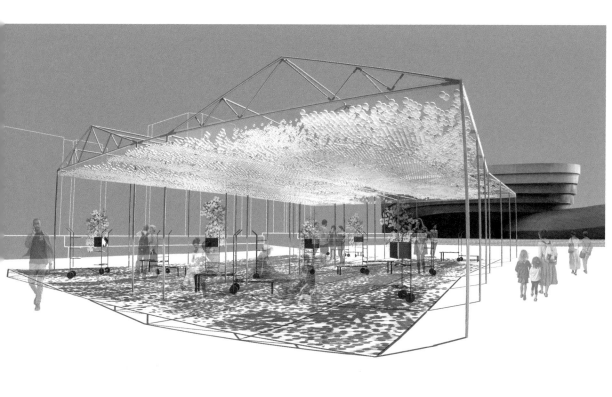

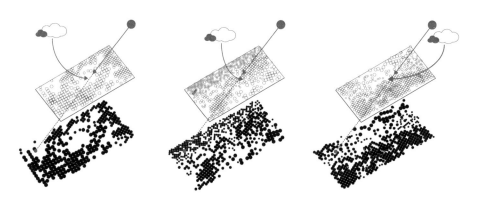

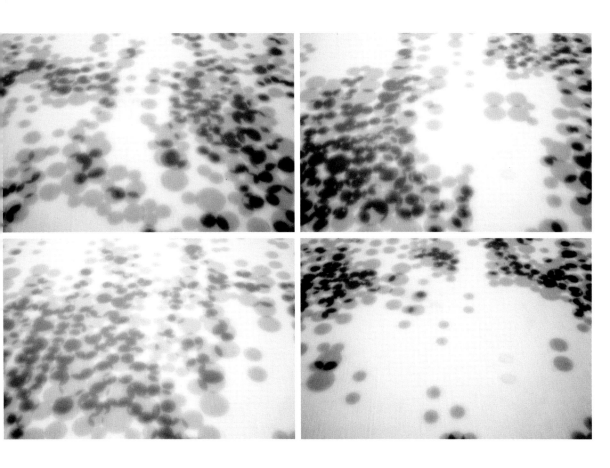

Above: Mock-up images; testing the moving shade from balls

Opposite above: The underutilized plaza is activated with public activities throughout the day

Opposite below: Urban shade based on both wind speed and sun orientation

Intake

Bridgeport, CT, US

Humid Subtropical Climate

Intake is an adaptive reuse of an abandoned shipbuilding factory located in Bridgeport, Connecticut. The city was historically a center for the shipbuilding and whaling industries. The design doubles the 50,000-square-foot factory into a 100,000-square-foot mixed-use facility. The existing ninety-foot-high structural frame is repurposed and expanded for additional programs. These include manufacturing, office, and educational and event programming, and foster interactions between employees and visitors. The building volumes are oriented in two directions—one visible from the commuter train station, the second providing views from the interior toward the water.

The existing interior, although flexible through its open space, is not conducive to the air quality control necessary for manufacturing. The design calls for subdividing with open walls and energy-efficient air curtains. These invisible "walls of air" control the spread of airborne pollutants without impeding the flow of people in the **limitless interior** of the facility. The air boundaries allow the creation of different zones, each with a distinct thermal experience (conditioned, partially conditioned, and unconditioned) without any visual separations. This creates a healthy work environment, improving productivity while reducing energy costs. Overlooking these open and interconnected areas are classrooms and event and exhibition spaces, which transform the industrial process into a public experience.

The revitalization of existing structures continues outdoors, where the industrial site becomes a publicly accessible waterfront park. The concrete paths and boat ramp along the water's edge have been converted into a scenic walking trail, enriched with lush, flood-resistant plantings. The centerpiece of the park is the "garden island," a calm and verdant space irrigated by rainwater collected by channels cut into the concrete slab of the former boat ramp.

Left: Aerial view of vacant warehouse and boat launching dock

Opposite: Interior of main hall indicating air curtains that provide thermal separation with visual connection

Intake

View from waterfront park toward
entrance with two building volumes

Intake

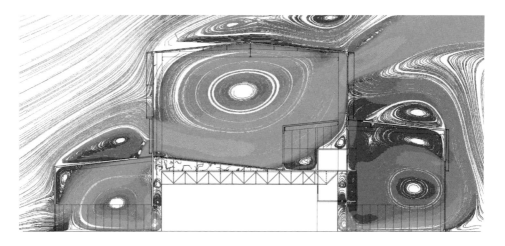

Pathline with Velocity

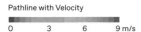

0   3   6   9 m/s

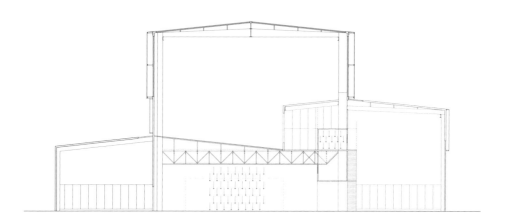

Above top: Computational fluid dynamic simulation of air velocity for mixed-mode ventilation

Above bottom: Building section indicating existing building and new construction

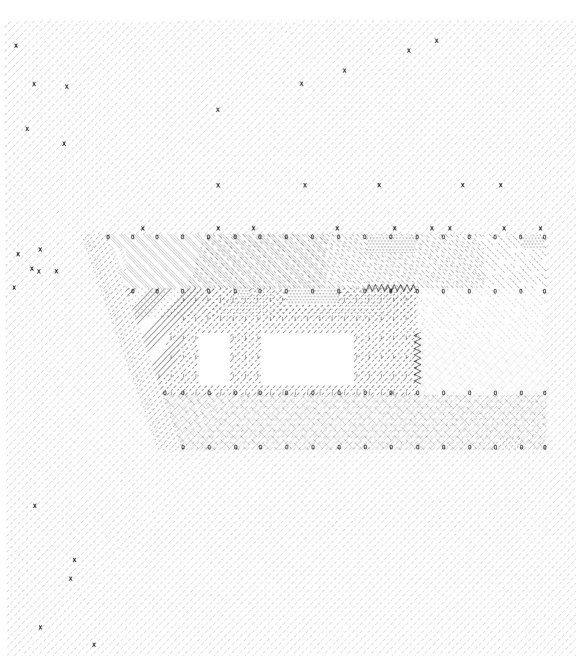

Level +0 climate plan; air curtains provide zones of thermal and air quality separation

Intake

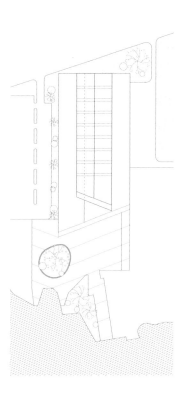

Above: Site plan, including garden island and waterfront promenade

Right: Aerial view, including boat dock to be rehabilitated into a waterfront park

Outdoor Room

Beijing, China

Humid Continental Climate

Outdoor Room was for the China International Architecture Biennial in Beijing's iconic Olympic Park, which has been massively underutilized since the completion of the 2008 Olympic Games. The plaza pavilion is a public meeting point, necessary within the open expanse of the park. Visitors wait to meet friends or simply rest on their way to an event in the National Stadium. The **outdoor interior** is diminutive within a vast urban scale, providing space for a quiet moment while at the same time bringing its surroundings within: both a room in the city and the city in the room.

The large-span steel structure is supported by "x-frame" walls with four perimeter columns, allowing for uninterrupted public space below. Gaps between fabric wall panels provide changing views to the park. The roof is composed of two large elliptical rings, interlocking one with the other and framing a large roof opening. Through this opening, views of the city continually materialize and dissolve in the sky depending on the air visibility.

The pavilion renders its surrounding environment; acting as a barometer of the air quality. On clear days, the roof opening frames the Olympic Observation Tower and beyond to the National Stadium. On days of low visibility, these landmarks disappear, swallowed by thick smog. Within the interior, the colors produced by air pollution—blues, grays, and beiges—are reflected and diffused by tensioned panels of white translucent fabric. *Outdoor Room* transforms the atmosphere into a mutating spectacle of the sky's changing colors, a **weather room** highlighting Beijing's worsening air quality conditions.

Above: View of pavilion on a day with low air quality

Opposite: Torqued fabric stretched from structural members form an open enclosure

Next: Views of landmarks through roof opening appear or disappear depending on air quality

Outdoor Room

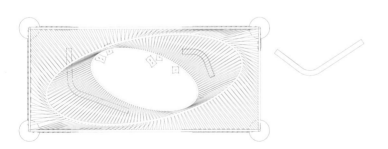

Above: Pavilion proposal with Beijing National Aquatics Center

Left above: Section through pavilion

Left below: Floor plan with ceiling above

Episode:
Weather Uncontrol

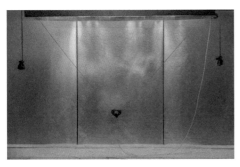

Weather Uncontrol was installed with the Storefront for Art and Architecture gallery a year after Hurricane Sandy. It revealed the invisible contaminants—silica, asbestos, and gypsum—that lingered in the air undetected, recasting the term "air rights" as an indoor health issue. Two robotic plotters generated static electric charges on a paper wall. The artificial dust released in the air clung to the charged paper, a process of **mechanical delirium** in which ephemeral dust drawings emerged slowly.

Above: Static electricity generator emits ions that attract artificial dust

Left above: Robotic plotter draws with static electricity and artificial dust to make wall-sized drawings, rendered visible with ultraviolet light

Left below: Visitors' air masks imprinted with quotes about air pollution and inequity of access to clean air

Heart Squared

New York City, US

US Humid Subtropical Climate

MODU and Eric Forman Studio

Heart Squared was a public artwork organized by Times Square Arts and curated by the Cooper Hewitt, Smithsonian Design Museum. Commissioned to celebrate love and diversity, *Heart Squared* evokes an abstracted anatomical heart out of an open steel lattice. A cloud of air, steel, and mirrors, it draws visitors to walk around it and experience an "infinite grid" in its kaleidoscopic reflections. Suspended within this colored steel lattice and angled in various directions, 125 mirrors reflect the surroundings of Times Square: people, buildings, billboards, and even the sky above.

When viewers find a particular location in the square, it reveals a large pixelated heart, surrounded by a field of reflected sky. Here, in one of the world's busiest public spaces, day or night, it is possible to connect to the sky above. *Heart Squared* is always changing

Left: A cloud of air, steel, and mirrors experienced in the round

Opposite: View from Father Duffy Square stairs

Heart Squared

with its surroundings—reflecting anyone who engages with it while providing momentary connections. The array of mirrors pixelates the built and natural environments: visitors from around the world, fragments of building exteriors, videos from billboards, and weather conditions in the sky.

Heart Squared prompts visitors to reconsider Times Square's verticality, focusing instead on the horizontal nature of its **public floor**. Crowded and active, New York's urban realm is integral to the city's identity. However, the installation achieves an unexpected quality: it is a quiet artwork amid a space of urban spectacle. The public's experience represents the collective heart of the city and, as such, is a civic statement about celebrating our differences and bringing people together in a fundamentally public manner.

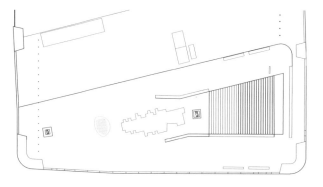

Above: Aerial view of public artwork

Left: Site plan; Father Duffy Square in Times Square

Above: Visitors interact with urban and
environmental surroundings

Below: View of "infinite grid" of reflected
images

Heart Squared

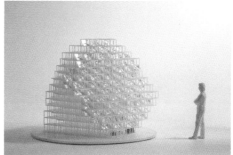

Above: Heart Squared changes in relation to its surroundings

Top right, bottom right: Model views of design proposal

Episode:
Field

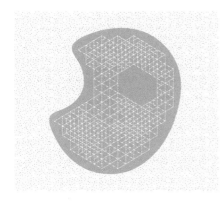

Field is a proposal for a slowly changing public artwork in Kyoto. The design evokes the experience of being surrounded by a natural field, a **crafted nature** highlighting the fragility and resilience of the environment. A viewing area allows visitors to be surrounded by the field of rods. The matrix of carbon-fiber rods, connected by flexible rubber joints, moves with the wind. The gentle movements change expression with daily wind patterns.

Top: Axonometric drawing; three-dimensional matrix of rods

Top Left: Floor plan with viewing area

Second Life

Location varies

Climate varies

Second Life transforms overlooked assets and vacant spaces in urban neighborhoods, revitalizing these properties for local communities. Our cities are home to countless properties that escape market demand for retrofit yet offer spaces for flexible use. Unlike traditional retrofits, *Second Life* focuses on the creation of "mini-buildings": free-standing, modular structures within empty buildings or open lots.

These mini-buildings utilize prefabricated components to optimize onsite assembly, significantly reducing the time and costs associated with building renovations. They are climatized independently and can be used "off the grid," enabling them to adapt to changing sites and weather. During cold weather, these

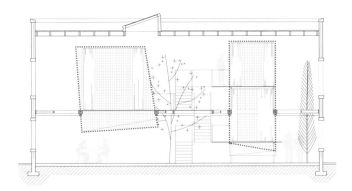

mini-buildings act as hubs of activity independent from each other. In temperate weather, they serve as "seeds" that grow to support more expansive activity. They have **dual futures**, with interim programming based on community needs and transitioning into long-term occupancy after an initial test period.

Second Life has two prototypes, the *Line* and the *Mat*, with thermal conditions suited to an existing building type and size. The *Line* is for sites like formerly industrial buildings or empty outdoor lots, used for local businesses or community groups. The modular structure supports transparent wall panels, which can be fully open or closed. Raised off the floor, the platform is passively cooled in warm months and independently climatized with radiant heating and thermal curtains in cold months.

The *Mat* is an approach to convert vacant homes for community use. It provides for conversion of these smaller buildings with inadequate structural integrity. A modular wood framing system stabilizes the existing structure and remains open-air. This floor framing is the structure supporting upper-level rooms. The rooms are enclosed in operable mesh metal panels that are semi-climatized like the *Line*.

Above: Building section; suspended "rooms" can be disassembled and moved to a different site

Left: An open ground floor provides gathering area for local businesses and community groups

Next: The *Line* prototype is enclosed with an open mesh for climbing plants

Second Life

Second Life

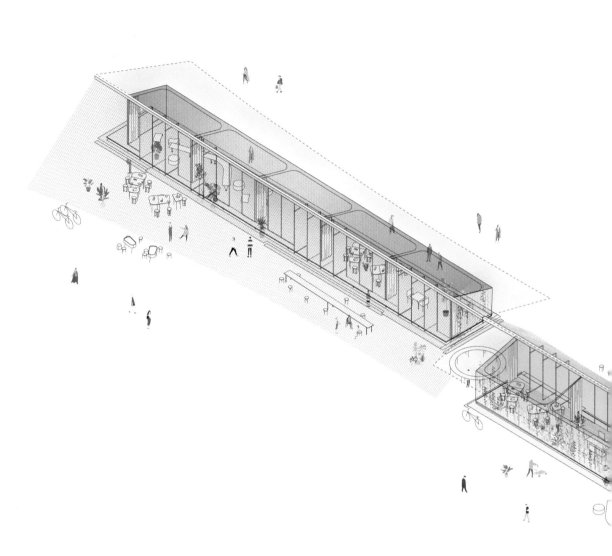

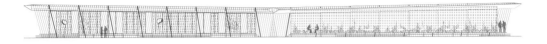

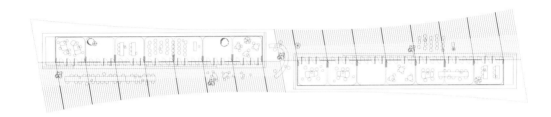

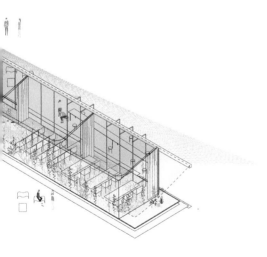

Above top: Elevation of the Line

Above bottom: Floor plan of the Line

Left: Axonometric; open canopies
extend into the existing building

Second Life

Mesh canopies create large areas
for gathering and provide for varied
programming

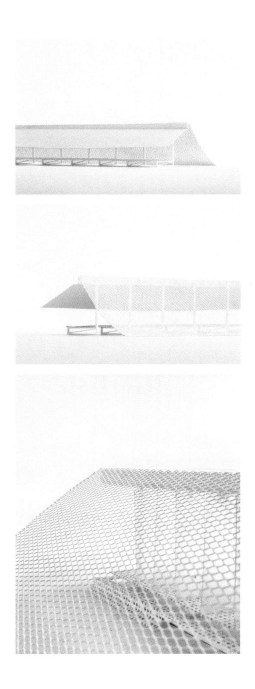

Above top: Radiant heating in roofs provide passive-energy heating and cooling

Above middle: Mesh canopies include water-misting systems for passive cooling as needed

Above bottom: The Line is an open-air structure that can also be enclosed for cooler weather

Second Life

Left: Young trees discovered inside a vacant property are supported by the Mat's open-floor structure

Below: Natural daylight is kept by passing through metal mesh panels

Episode:
Platform

Platform is an open-air building reimagining an incomplete train station on the outskirts of Milan. It gives a new future to the station, a **memoryless ruin** designed by Aldo Rossi, transforming it into a place for work and learning. Its occupants interact in an environment that is part workspace and part urban plaza. The city's temperate climate allows for an open building envelope, making it possible to work indoors while experiencing the outdoors. Microclimate design strategies such as interior gardens and radiant-heated furniture offer thermal diversity in adaptable spaces.

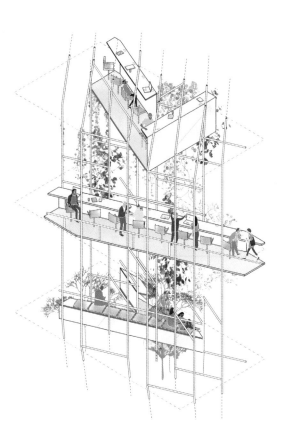

Opposite: Radiant furniture provides passive-energy heating in the Tower of Air's semi-exterior areas

Above: An incomplete train station transformed into an open-air building for work and learning

Mapping:
Urban Voids

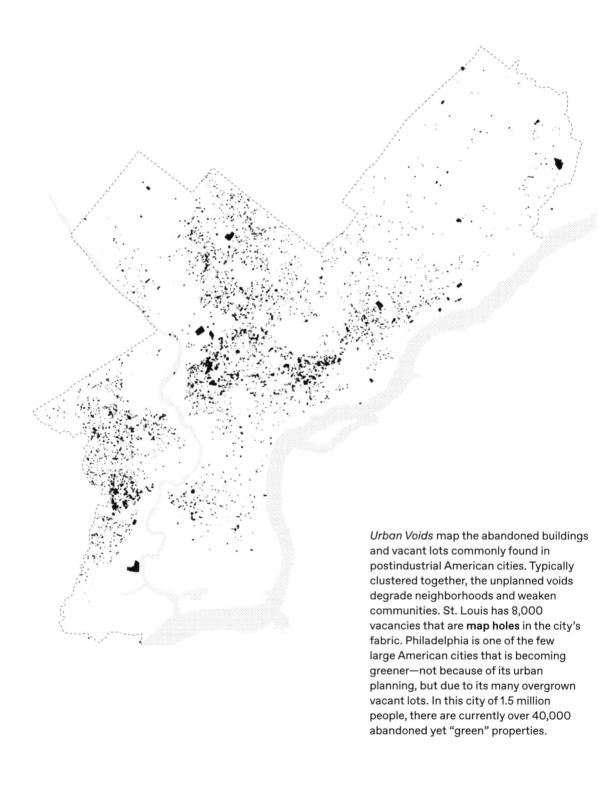

Urban Voids map the abandoned buildings
and vacant lots commonly found in
postindustrial American cities. Typically
clustered together, the unplanned voids
degrade neighborhoods and weaken
communities. St. Louis has 8,000
vacancies that are **map holes** in the city's
fabric. Philadelphia is one of the few
large American cities that is becoming
greener—not because of its urban
planning, but due to its many overgrown
vacant lots. In this city of 1.5 million
people, there are currently over 40,000
abandoned yet "green" properties.

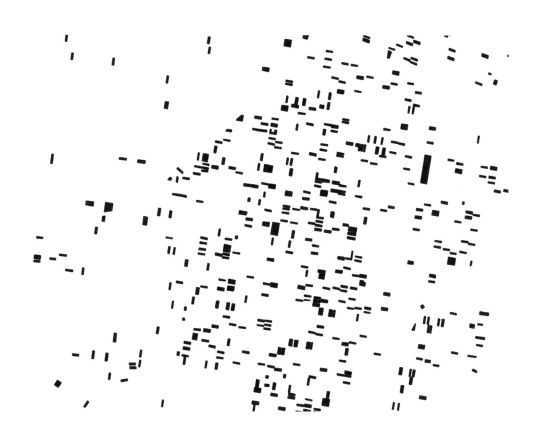

Above: Philadelphia's 40,000
abandoned buildings and vacant lots

Right: City property map

Opposite: Philadelphia is one of the few
cities becoming greener from overgrown
vacant lots

Incomplete Whole

Recording: Incomplete City
Episode: Disappearing Ruins
Episode: Flexing Structures
Incomplete Whole: Urban Exploration in Italy

Recording:
Incomplete City

San Cristoforo train
station, Milan

San Cristoforo train
station, Milan

Città dello Sport Tor Vergata
natatorium, Rome

Città dello Sport Tor Vergata
natatorium, Rome

Above: Polo Stadium,
Giarre

Below: Città dello Sport Tor
Vergata natatorium, Rome

Opposite: Housing,
Gibellina Nuova

Theater, Gibellina Nuova

Above: Theater, Gibellina Nuova

Opposite: Grande Hotel de
Calogero, Sciacca

Episode:
Disappearing Ruins

Above: Dual atmospheres of Piazza del Popolo

Opposite: Dual atmospheres of Collona Antonina

Disappearing Ruins are collages reimagining Giovanni Battista Piranesi's "Vedute di Roma" as invisible atmospheres, both meteorological and experiential. Archival research of the print editions reveals a process of reetching copper engraving plates over decades. Changing only two areas—the clouds above and the ground shade below—Piranesi rarely made changes to the architecture. The drawings reveal through subtraction, removing architecture to focus on weather, climate, and experience. Since Piranesi lived at the end of the Little Ice Age, perhaps he was depicting **weather memories** of climate change?

1. Palazzo Chigi
2. Piazza Colonna

Colonna Antonina

3. Strada del Corso

Episode:
Flexing Structures

Above: Flexing Structures move with environmental forces

Opposite: Mock-up of Flexing Structures tests carbon-fiber material

Flexing Structures is a research initiative investigating carbon-fiber structures that are adaptable to environmental phenomena. Carbon fiber is ten times stronger than steel, and five times lighter. The structural prototype is composed of a lattice of interlinked rods reacting to—rather than resisting—the forces of wind. While traditional structural systems are designed to be "hard" enough to resist dynamic wind forces, carbon fiber presents opportunities to incorporate **flexible gaps** in structures that are resilient through their flexibility.

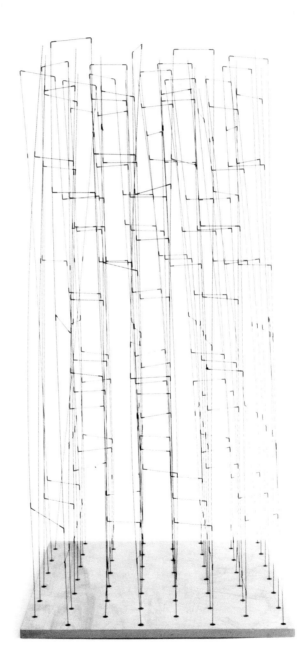

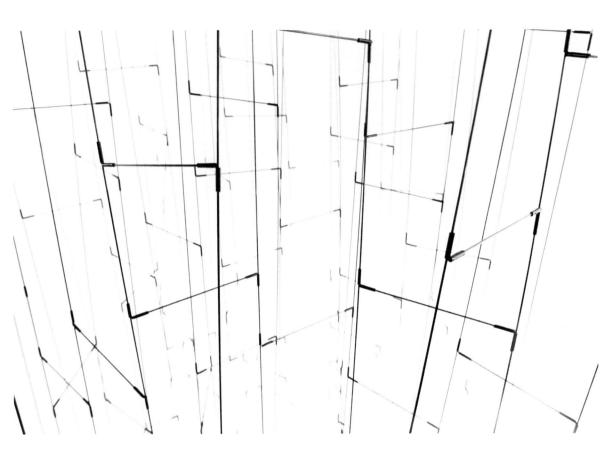

Above: A lattice of structural rods
connected with flexible joints

Opposite: Flexing Structure in
movement

Incomplete Whole:
Urban Exploration in Italy

Rachely Rotem with Phu Hoang

An incomplete whole is a modern ruin. It is a building or infrastructure that never completed construction. Decades have passed, and its original use has been forgotten. They are open shells scattered in the cities and landscapes of many places, from China's "ghost cities" to Africa's "new towns." They can be found especially in southern Europe—many in Italy, Spain, Greece, and Portugal—after the 2008 global economic crisis halted their construction.[1] From northern to southern Italy, there are hundreds of incomplete structures built mostly over the past thirty years. Italy's long history of living with ruins offers opportunities to rethink their futures.[2]

An incomplete whole is financial malfeasance. Italy had two periods of accelerated growth. The first, its "boom years," was part of the country's postwar building expansion; the second was in early 2000, when Italy received loans from the EU to finance a wide array of programs.[3] Once European Union funding stopped in 2008, many speculative projects across the region were affected. The situation was made worse by a legal loophole: construction bids are not legal obligations, and contractors can present a low bid to be awarded a project but increase the cost afterward.[4] This led to a building culture of cost overruns—or worse, projects that were never meant to be completed. Santiago Calatrava's La Città dello Sport (2005) in Rome was intended to be a sports facility for the 2009 World Swimming Competition but was halted in 2012 when its costs doubled.

Above: Città dello Sport Tor Vergata, Rome; thermal photography indicating sunlit spaces during winter

An incomplete whole is a political game. Sicily, with Italy's highest concentration of incomplete structures, has an extremely high youth unemployment rate. Rather than responding directly to a community's needs, sometimes a public project is built simply to reduce the unemployment rate.[5] Speculative urbanization became a temporary driver of growth until funds ran out. The politics of securing votes for building initiatives that were never intended to be completed created entire towns in a continual state of incompletion. The Sicilian town of Giarre is the most poignant example. The municipality received European Union funds to build a polo stadium, though it is not played locally.[6] The dimensions of a polo field made it impossible to adapt the space to more commonly played sports, such as soccer, though this was never questioned.

An incomplete whole is a microclimate. It is mild relative to its outdoor surroundings. Evaluating it through its passive performance qualifies it

as an environmental infrastructure. The incomplete structures dominate Sicily's landscape as a network of shaded relief from the extreme sun. Its form changes with the light, softening its volumetric intensity. Natural breezes funnel through many apertures and voids, while the thermal mass, with its abundance of concrete, collects the sun's energy throughout the day and releases it at night. In locations in northern Italy, such as the incomplete San Cristoforo station in Milan, shallow floor slab depths allow for solar radiation to enter deep into the space and warm it during the wintertime when the sun angle is lower.

Above top: Polo Stadium, Giarre; stairs for people and plants

Above bottom: Polo stadium, Giarre; children playing between indoors and outdoors.

An incomplete whole is an environmental study. It rethinks the traditional role of architecture as a shelter from the environment. Traditionally, the building envelope is the threshold between exterior and interior, public and private. It is also a border between outdoor and conditioned indoor. It is a costly border, as it perpetuates our dependency on fossil fuel energy to provide an optimized indoor climate. This creates a devastating loop of ever-increasing urban heat islands, a consequence of removing heat from the indoors to the outdoors and our further dependency on artificial cooling of the indoors. The environmental border of an incomplete structure becomes diffuse as planned windows and doors were never installed. It is an **outdoor interior**, neither indoors—as it is mostly open-air—nor outdoors, as it is mostly covered. Thus, it is both artificial and natural, as well as simultaneously urban, architectural, and landscape.

An Incomplete whole is an antitype. Its intended building type—bridge, hotel, stadium, swimming pool, museum, theater, and railway station—

was defined, but its present conditions escape classifications based on use. In 1968, an earthquake destroyed the Sicilian town of Gibellina, which prompted the construction of Nuova Gibellina in an alternate location. The old town was memorialized in Land Art that buried its ruins in concrete. *Cretto di Burri*, by Alberto Burri, took over thirty years to complete.[7] Nuova Gibellina was built from barren land with buildings

designed by the prominent Italian architects Vittorio Gregotti, Franco Purini, and Ludovico Quaroni. However, there were too many civic buildings planned for a town of less than 5,000 people. A town hall, museum, sports facilities, cathedral, and five piazzas all turned into open-air structures that collectively form a city in a pending state.[8]

Above Top: Città dello Sport Tor Vergata, Rome; birds occupying incomplete structures

Above bottom: Plants growing in gaps between building elements

An Incomplete whole is an anti-monument. The ambitions of designers, while never realized, are evident in the partial construction of an idiosyncratic form and structure. Never occupied and without a history of collective memory, it lacks the nostalgia of an abandoned ruin. The incomplete San Cristoforo train station, on the outskirts of Milan, was designed by Aldo Rossi and Gianni Braghieri using signifiers of past ruins; meanwhile, it is in a constant state of ruination. A monument suggests a process of selecting memory and meaning, a place that retains references of past times—this process was evident in Rossi's projects and writing.[9] By contrast, the anti-monument is a result of natural forces erasing the significance of past cultural symbols, producing a place in constant fluctuation depending on the day's weather forecast.

An incomplete whole is a free place. It is a site of **occasional architecture**. Inherently public, it contains no borders and is yet exempt from societal expectations, which were never formally established in it. It is not connected to urban grids and is often remote from cellular towers, allowing it to be in a rare state of being unsurveyed. It creates an opportunity for new subcultures to congregate and emerge. Graffiti marks voices and opinions on walls as acts of civic defiance. The lack of interior finishes gives it an atmosphere of carefree use. A group of school children in Sicily's Giarre turned the polo stadium's shell into their own club, where they played an unusual form of soccer, kicking the balls through holes in the walls between rooms.

An incomplete whole is non-design. It lets nature lead in place-making by prompting more biodiversity. Over time, it becomes an infrastructure of **wild urbanism**. In Rome's La Città dello Sport, nature enters as the architecture deteriorates. The process of ruination is alive. An ecological cycle begins as dust settles and wild seeds land within, carried by birds that find temporary refuge within the structure. Raindrops channel a pass through the cracks of concrete slabs, and soft greenery starts to grow—first within the boundaries of the cracks, and then expanding beyond. Small animals find refuge within this young ecology, bringing more wildlife indoors. Over time, it becomes a place of mixed environments, where architecture and nature merge through a continuous process of change.

An incomplete whole is a state of mind. As a process of ruination continues, the prospect of architectural completion, in a traditional sense, becomes more financially challenging. Yet one can accept this incompleteness as its inherent character. It is an architecture apart from property claims and the powers they represent, as it is typologically undefined, its borders are ever-changing, and its users are multispecies. It is an architecture of impact: a place for the temporary, for the unheard, for the voices of the moment and the future. A place to fulfill interim needs and scenarios rather than a fixed resolution or set program. It is an infrastructure to challenge **second nature**—an opportunity to unlearn how to separate ourselves from the natural world and from each other.

1. Chris Marcinkoski, *The City That Never Was* (New York, 2016).

2. Iñaqui Carnicero, "Architecture Non Finito," in *Unfinished* (Barcelona/Madrid, 2016).

3. Stacy Meichtry, "Sicilian Town's Woes Show European Waste," *The Wall Street Journal*, October 22, 2012.

4. Alan Johnston, "Italy Planning Fiasco: New Ruins Litter Sicily," BBC News, May 18, 2012.

5. Rachel Donadio, "Corruption Is Seen as a Drain on Italy's South," *The New York Times*, October 8, 2012.

6. Peter Popham, "Concrete Jungle: How Italy's Modern Ruins Became Art," *Independent*, August 8, 2010.

7. Angela Maderna, "In Gibellina the Cretto by Burri Is Finished (after 30 Years)," *Abitare*, November 6, 2015.

8. Patricia Zohn, "The Art of Recovery: How a Radical Public Art Experiment is Reshaping Sicily 50 Years After a Devastating Earthquake," *Artnet*, August 15, 2018.

9. Aldo Rossi, *The Architecture of the City* (Cambridge, MA, 1984).

Città dello Sport Tor Vergata
natatorium, Rome

Projects

Mini Tower One

New York City, US

Humid Subtropical Climate

Mini Tower One is an addition to the rear of a two-family Brooklyn townhouse. The project extends the use of each home by providing space for combined activities. Each floor of the townhouse is enlarged, adding areas for work and learning. Several areas are **outdoor interiors**, such as an indoor terrace to an all-season room. They can be enclosed so residents can experience seasons passing, viewing summer rains or winter snowfalls.

Living in *Mini Tower One* connects residents to urban nature, incorporating low-energy strategies to improve both indoor and outdoor comfort. An "indoor tree" provides air filtration and cooler microclimates, while radiant outdoor heating extends the use of the indoor terrace. A mechanical air curtain allows the all-weather room to be open to the outdoors while maintaining interior environments. The roof terrace includes both an edible garden and a shading canopy. The addition's exterior cladding is limited to two materials: folded metal panels and perforated versions of those panels.

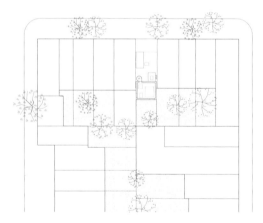

Left: Site plan, urban infill lots with rear yard

Right: A series of indoor/outdoor spaces connected vertically

The project is a passive house with a high-performance building envelope to reduce energy use. However, during temperate seasons, large openings promote indoor-outdoor living, seemingly in contradiction to passive house design. In fact, the townhouse is airtight during peak heating and cooling seasons but open to the outdoors in temperate weather. During this time, passive cooling through a roof fan allows cross-ventilation of all rooms— reinventing the Brooklyn townhouse, with its narrow and deep lots, as an open-air **season house**.

Mini Tower One

Above: Mesh metal stair passes light from skylight above

Opposite top: Section; showing enlargement of each floor and adding an additional floor

Opposite bottom left: Model view of rear garden

Opposite bottom right: Model view of terrace with edible roof garden

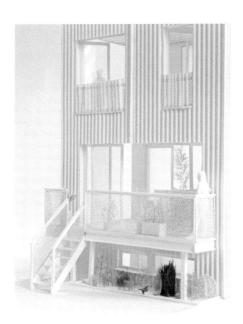
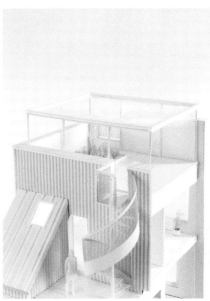

Mini Tower One

Above: Mirrors surround opening between existing and new building

Right: Mirror reflects image of a tall birch tree outdoors

Opposite: Light passing through upper townhouse unit

Mini Tower One

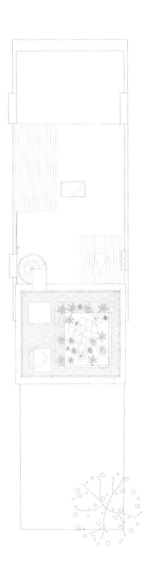

Above: Floor plans; three spaces
in-between indoor and outdoor

Opposite: Aluminum cladding reflects
light in two directions

Mini Tower One

Above: A passive house open to outdoors
during temperate seasons

Opposite: A mini tower in Brooklyn

Episode:
Psychometric Thresholds

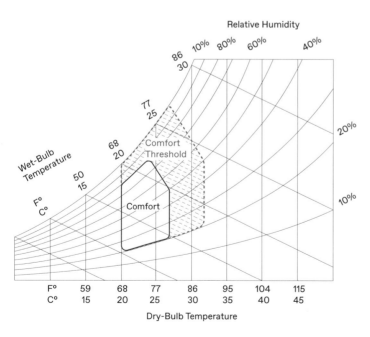

Relative Humidity

Wet-Bulb
Temperature

Comfort
Threshold

Comfort

| F° | 59 | 68 | 77 | 86 | 95 | 104 | 115 |
| C° | 15 | 20 | 25 | 30 | 35 | 40 | 45 |

Dry-Bulb Temperature

Psychometric Thresholds simultaneously improves both outdoor and indoor comfort. Rather than focus on the central comfort zone of the American Society of Heating, Refrigerating and Air-Conditioning Engineer (ASHRAE) psychometric chart, its surrounding regions are highlighted as important spatial thresholds. These areas can preheat or precool outdoor air before it enters the building or contacts the building envelope. *Mini Tower One*'s threshold spaces of **outdoor interiors**—from an indoor terrace to an all-weather room—mitigate air temperature and reduces energy use while also creating experiences between indoor and outdoor environments.

Above: Semi-exterior indoor terrace is a thermal threshold for interiors

Left: Psychometric chart reinterpreted for comfort threshold area

Opposite: Indoor/outdoor wall section, showing space for indoor tree

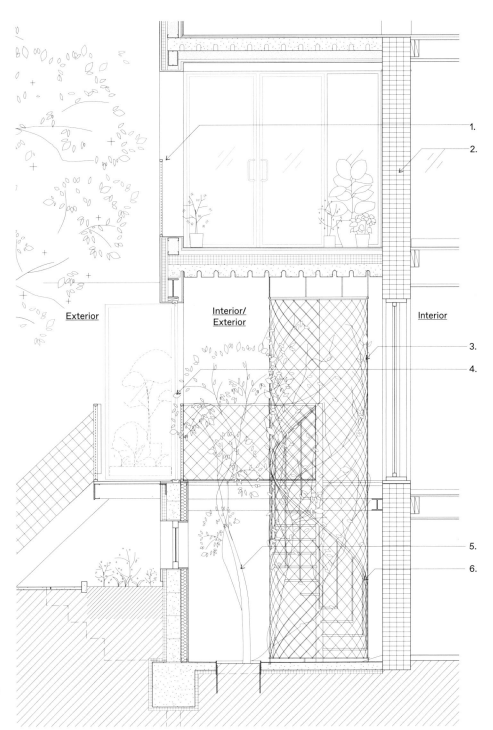

Exterior

Interior/
Exterior

Interior

1. Indoor Terrace Railing
2. Existing Masonry Wall
3. Plant Growing Mesh
4. Accordion Glass Doors
5. Indoor Tree
6. Metal Spiral Stair

Mapping:
Mini Towers

Lot Types (Brooklyn)

■ Corner lots

■ Inside lots

Lot Depth (Queens)

■ Lots less than 90'

■ Lots less than 70'

Above left: Zoning map of Brooklyn
lot types

Above right: Zoning map of Queens
lot depth

Opposite: Urban map of Brooklyn
lot types

Mini Towers map lots in the boroughs of
Brooklyn and Queens that are irregularities
in New York City's Zoning Resolution. They
occur from anomalies in urban growth and
are addressed through zoning exemptions,
creating rules from exceptions. Each lot
has additional buildable area; they are small
footprints but with vertical opportunity.
Together, these vertical slices of zoning
opportunities constitute a **small vastness**,
rear-yard "mini towers" of stacked rooms
forming an urban network mostly hidden
from public view.

Promenade

Houston, US

Humid Subtropical Climate

Promenade is a mixed-use office and retail center in Houston. Each unit includes a shaded exterior area, providing access to gardens and extending the indoor activities of work and retail outdoors. These areas are set at an angle to the street, increasing both visibility and view. The second-story building volume is angled similarly. These areas, as well as the second-floor terrace, invite both visitors and employees—**familiar strangers**—to gather and socialize.

Promenade is tailored for Houston's hot climate with passive design strategies that reduce energy use and provide outdoor experiences. Self-cooling facades, tall aluminum shading "fins," and overhanging trellises improve comfort. The self-cooling concrete walls are cast with patterns that, when passed over by wind, dissipate solar heat more quickly. These architectural elements create cool microclimates for gathering while establishing an architectural identity for the center. Around each entrance, the "fins" provide shade as they rise from the gardens; some include mesh material for climbing plants that create an additional microclimate.

People stroll along gardens planted from different local ecologies: a Texas rock garden, a tall grass garden, a garden for pollinators, and a desert garden. *Promenade* connects work and retail to multi-sensorial outdoor environments, from the fragrant scent of jasmine climbers to the shade from bamboo groves. The result is part architecture, part nature—combined for improved comfort in a hot climate.

Left: Recessed areas provide gathering areas for visitors and employees

Right: Bamboo and jasmine climbers create cooler areas

Promenade

Above: Two directions of building orientation toward street

Right: Shading fins at varying distances from wall

Opposite top: Shading canopies vary along entrance wall

Opposite bottom: Indoor/outdoor wall section, showing recessed areas with gardens

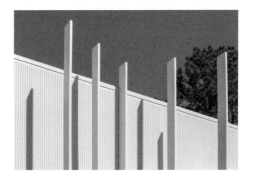

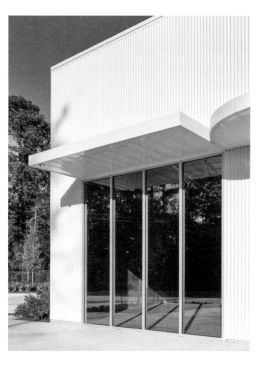

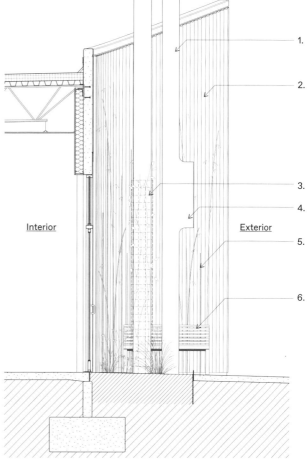

1. Aluminum Shading Fin
2. Patterned Concrete Wall
3. Plant Growing Screen
4. Integrated Signage
5. Bamboo Planting
6. Outdoor Seating

Interior

Exterior

1.
2.
3.
4.
5.
6.

Promenade

Above, top: Low, horizontal building
surrounded by trees

Above, right: Ground-floor plan

Opposite: Pergola supported by
structural fins

Promenade

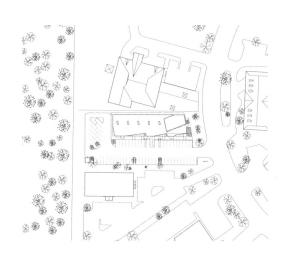

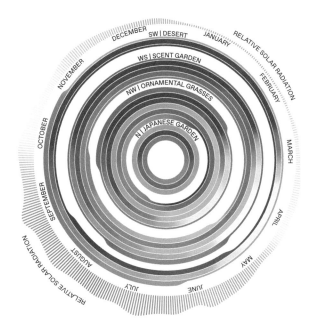

Opposite: Upper level includes an outdoor terrace

Above, top: Site plan showing relationship to the street

Above, bottom: Diagram of seasonal plantings with building solar radiation

Above: Shading pergola from below

Opposite top, bottom: Model views of
design proposal

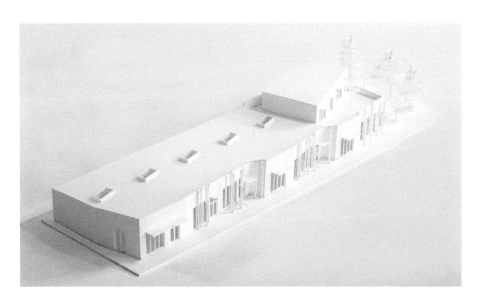

Promenade

Patterned and curved walls indicate
recessed areas

Episode:
Self-Cooling Walls

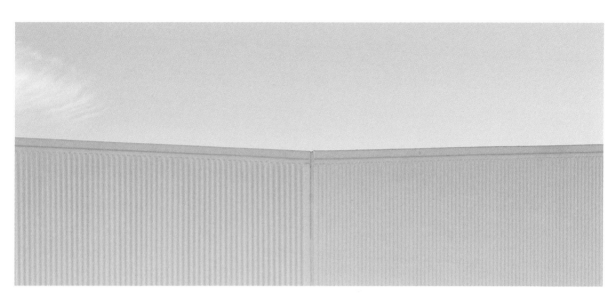

Above top: Variations in corrugation patterns result in different cooling rates

Above bottom: Two different corrugation patterns used for building envelope

Opposite: Thermal studies; different corrugation patterns release heat at different rates

Self-Cooling Walls is a building envelope designed for improved outdoor comfort. White concrete reflects sunlight while cast corrugated patterns release solar heat. The concrete patterns, when combined with wind, release heat quicker than flat panels. Tests using thermal photography were conducted with heated panels of different patterns; **digital weather** results showed a fifteen-degree surface temperature difference. A panel with 70 percent more surface area only increased mass by 6 percent, allowing it to release heat more efficiently and economically.

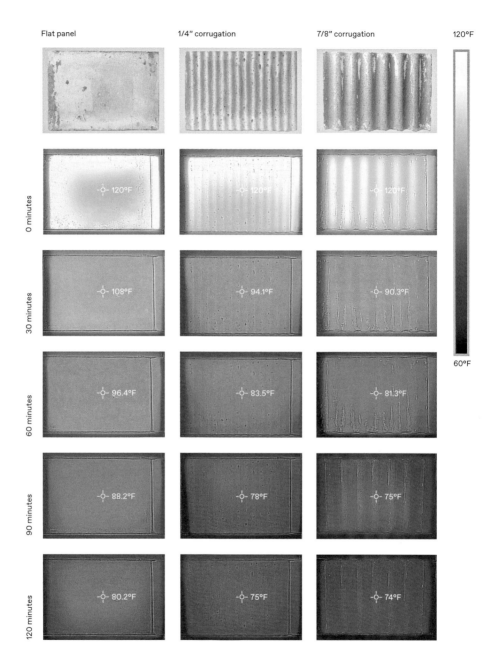

Double House

Double House consists of two townhouses designed for a mother and her adult daughter. The multigenerational home is divided by a wall but connected twice, both outside and inside. In the rear yard, patios are linked through a shared garden—a space for **hearing plants**. On the top floor, the townhouses share an indoor-outdoor "bridge room." This multifunctional and adaptable space is accessible from both units, and can be used as an indoor terrace, remote office, or home gym. The project is two homes together, yet separate.

Situated on a corner lot, the building volume of *Double House* has angled walls for two orientations. Recessed volumes provide shade, and the white metal exterior reflects extreme solar heat. Daily indoor activities occur in areas located for the changing light of the day. The kitchen receives low morning sun, while the living room provides an afternoon view over downtown Houston. The dining area invites dusk views of tree canopies. These daily rituals are also reflected in the building envelope. Rather than a repetition of windows, different sizes and heights capture views of nearby trees and the city skyline while also providing privacy from neighbors.

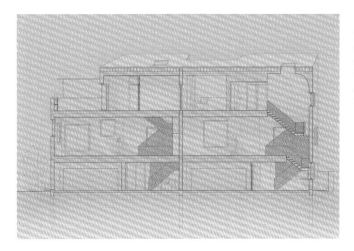

Left: Thermal microclimates during summer season

Opposite top: Axonometric; semi-exterior areas combine shade with plantings to improve outdoor comfort

Opposite bottom: Section; showing indoor-outdoor areas

Houston's hot climate calls for improving both indoor and outdoor comfort. The third floor incorporates large operable walls, and its terraces have deep roof overhangs and trellises for shade. The staircase incorporates a large operable skylight at the top to let in natural light for all three floors. The skylight is operable to evacuate hot air from each floor, providing ventilation during temperate weather. Rear patios are recessed to provide shade, while the front yard includes natural meadows with resilient plantings that serve as rain gardens for Houston's heavy rains.

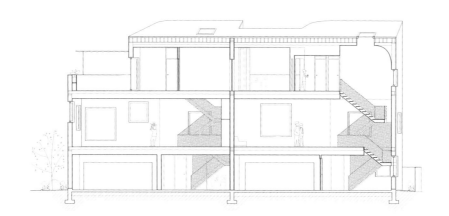

Double House

The townhouses are separate yet
connected through indoor-outdoor areas

Double House

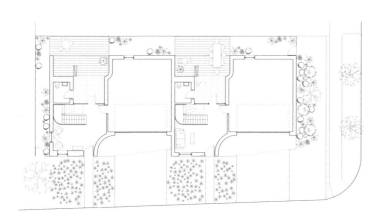

Above: Floor plans; ground-floor all-season rooms and upper-floor "bridge room" are adaptable for different seasons and uses

Opposite above: Interior of second-floor level with windows located for interior activities and exterior surroundings

Opposite below: Recessed patios provide shade for Houston's hot climate

Exhale

Miami Beach, US

Tropical Climate

Exhale was an art park hosted by the contemporary art fair company Art Basel Miami Beach and by Creative Time, a New York public arts organization. The 25,000-square-foot underutilized beach plot in Miami Beach was transformed into a performance art venue for events and performances. The public was invited to programs curated by collaborating arts organizations based in Detroit, Mexico City, Berlin, and Glasgow. The park eschewed static divisions of space, instead promoting constant activity in open spaces that organizations selected based on their performances.

Performance areas ranged from the formal, such as the outdoor stage, to the informal, including clearings in the sand and hammock groves. During films, dances, DJ sets, and concerts, an undulating rope canopy overhead changed with daily wind conditions. Seven miles of draping ropes moved in the wind, resulting in a dynamic environment. Wind is inherently without form, and the **occasional architecture** of the art park harnessed this inherent formlessness to create an interactive environment for performance art.

Left: Dance performances occur in open areas without formal stages

Opposite: Rope canopies suspended from steel structures are for both performers and members of the public

The ropes swayed in the wind, creating active spaces that changed in shape and use over time. These variable spaces encouraged impromptu interactions between members of the public and performance artists, who together interacted with the wind. At night, structures as high as forty feet were illuminated with lighting, programmed to respond to changes in the wind's speed—producing an interplay between performance, public, and the environment.

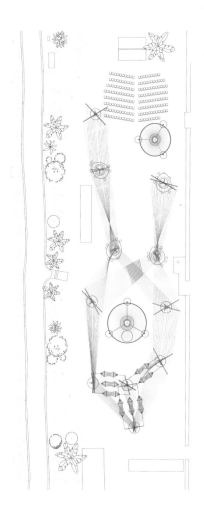

Above: Site plan of beachfront site

Left: Opening night of the art park during the Art Basel Miami Beach contemporary art fair

Exhale

Seven miles of rope were used for the
art park

Episode:
Coral Footings

Coral Footings are underwater structures designed for artificial coral reefs. All the construction materials of *Exhale* were recycled. The unpainted steel structures were returned to a foundry and the rope was donated to local schools. The concrete footings were given to the Florida Department of Environmental Protection and repurposed for their artificial coral reef program. The design of the footings included holes and texture to promote coral growth, and diverse marine life has slowly developed—a **memoryless ruin** below the water surface.

Above: Concrete structural footings were donated to build artificial coral reefs

Left top: Concrete texture was specified to promote coral reef growth

Left bottom: Footings were designed with holes to foster marine life

Habits and Habitats

Jackson Hole, WY, US

Continental Subarctic Climate

Habits and Habitats is a nature observatory, sited within thirty acres in the Greater Yellowstone ecology of Jackson Hole. The migratory corridor of the Snake River brings wildlife close to people, with elk, moose, deer, and bears nearby. Visitors come to the observatory to experience wildlife in their natural habitat. This experience is immersive rather than distanced, as the observatory allows for the study of wildlife with a connection to the outdoors.

The observatory is a mass timber structure clad with stone and wood. It is a net-zero-energy building that also meets passive house building standards, while also enabling seasonal connections to the outdoors. An all-weather room provides visitors with experiences of thermal diversity. This room, open to the outdoors during the

winter, includes hot and cold plunge pools. During inclement weather, the adaptable room is closed to the exterior and open to the interior, with a sauna and a fireplace for gathering. The pools, sauna, and radiant heating use geothermal wells.

The design includes several semi-exterior areas—two wildlife blinds, a covered viewing deck, and a roof terrace—that connect architecture with its surrounding environment. The blinds provide screening to view wildlife, such as **bird companions**, and includes pollinating gardens that attract local birds. The covered deck frames an uninterrupted view of the Teton Range. A raised walkway connects walking paths to the deck and the terrace, weaving through tree groves with a reading area surrounded by foliage. It is both an immersive nature observatory and a restorative retreat.

Above: Section through building and landscape

Left: Nature observatory for immersive experiences

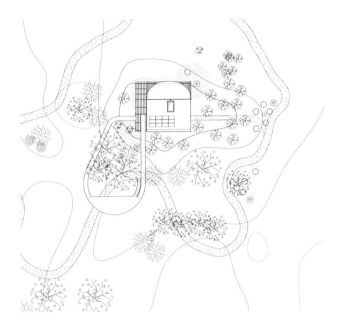

Above: Site plan showing walking paths connected to deck and terrace

Left: Raised walkway from viewing deck to roof terrace

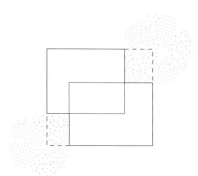

Above: Floor plan showing
all-weather room

Left: Diagram of environmental
strategy

Above, left: Model views of proposal

Above: View toward Teton Range from viewing deck and pool

Left: Operable doors can connect all-weather room to interior and exterior

Opposite: Indoor/outdoor section, showing all-weather room with plunge pool

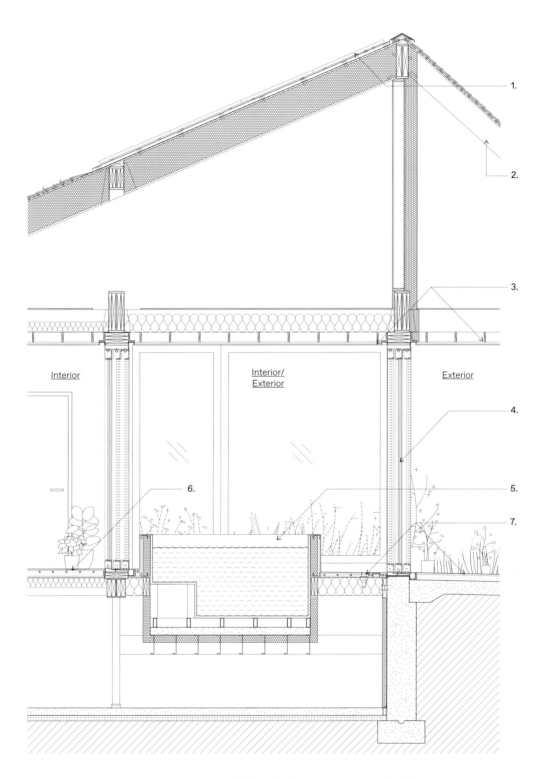

Interior

Interior/
Exterior

Exterior

1.
2.
3.
4.
5.
6.
7.

1. Photovoltaic Panels
2. Wood Rafters
3. Continuous Oak Wood Ceiling
4. Operable Glass Doors

5. Hot Spa Pool
6. Radiant Stone Floor
7. Continuous Slate Flooring

Second Nature

Fumihiko Maki
Itsuko Hasegawa
Kengo Kuma
Ryue Nishizawa
Takaharu and Yui Tezuka
Go Hasegawa
Second Nature: Conversations in Tokyo

Conversation:
Fumihiko Maki

Rachely Rotem (RR): Let's start at the beginning: Why did you start your own architecture practice?

Fumihiko Maki (FM): In high school, I was interested in designing model airplanes and building them to fly. I thought I might become an aeronautic engineer. When World War II ended, that opportunity disappeared. I was still interested in making things, though, so I went into architecture.

RR: Speaking of making things, how do you start designing a project?

FM: After I went to architecture school, I spent some time in Tange's studio. His method was to give us a theme and then have each of us debate with him—on a number of occasions—until we gradually developed ideas from that original concept. The final decision was always his to make, but I learned from Tange that the process was very important.

This is particularly true when we face complex architectural problems. Even in free discussions among ourselves, identifying the theme becomes very important: What is it for a particular project? We still practice that way now—with open discussions to arrive at a theme.

RR: Speaking of openness, "open linkage" was part of your idea of group form—links that are both unit and system, open-ended within its own boundaries.

FM: Yes, because I don't have a particular style. I think architecture should be for users as much as for clients. Sometimes there are bad clients, and if we follow their instructions, the results can be disastrous. Fortunately, I have not had any bad clients. Regardless, though, architecture is for society. That is my philosophy.

RR: Was group form an idea of architecture for society?

FM: Group form developed out of my experiences early in my career, when I visited villages in other places around the world. I began to see through the disorganization and identified the informal spatial systems that have developed over time. I became interested in how and why they came to be.

It is one of three collective forms that have interested me in my writing. I have tried to objectively analyze and evaluate the existence of the three fundamental collective forms. Group form is only one of these three types of collective form. Besides group form, you have compositional form and mega-form. In the 1960s, mega-forms were very popular. Even great architects used them— like Le Corbusier's "Obus" in Algiers, Tange's "A Plan for Tokyo," and Yona Friedman in France.

RR: So, collective forms began as a body of research that became design methodologies?

FM: When you design a university campus you need some kind of collective form. Whether it is group form, compositional form, or it could be mega-form, in the end it all depends on the theme. In our design for the Republic Polytechnic in Singapore, the campus has all three kinds of collective form. There is one huge mega-form where students spend their days, small sorts of spaces where students make their own places, and then outside spaces for different kinds of use, such as a gymnasium and housing and so on. The design of the Republic Polytechnic campus plan reflects all three of those collective forms, so it is not just an example of group form.

The space in between buildings, which we call linkage, is also very important. When I designed three campuses with nothing around them, the question was how to make collective form. I am also often asked to design a single building on existing campuses, whether at the University of Pennsylvania or at Washington University. In those cases, the question is how you can make an element within an existing collective form. It all depends on the project.

Phu Hoang (PH): Mega-forms can result in vast urban spaces while group form humanizes this large scale.

FM: Yes, but when we did the Keio University campus in Fujisawa, our first campus planning project, the client asked us to build villages rather than huge mega-forms. So, the client already didn't like this dehumanizing tendency of mega-forms, which at the time was popular in other Japanese universities. Of course, I was very sympathetic to that theme—the idea of villages—and it was precisely what we wanted to do. In that case, the approach came from the client.

RR: At Hillside Terrace, you designed for opposing scales: a very large urban scale and an extra-small scale, such as designing for the space of a tree and its shade.

FM: Yes.

RR: How do the two scales—the urban scale and the scale of a tree—coexist?

FM: I'll give you an example of one very particular morphological principal in Japanese cities. Large streets are usually lined with high-rises. Those streets are high-density, but the internal streets are left to be more human scale. This is because in Japan, the floor–area ratio and maximum building height are determined by how wide the street is. So, when the street is narrow, one cannot build more than ten meters high.

However, Hillside Terrace was unique, because while the street width allows for buildings to be twenty-two meters high, it has developed in a unique combination of wide streets and low-rise developments. That's because the landowner of the area, during the beginning of the Showa period, said, "Tokyo should have wider streets; up until now these streets have been very narrow." So, he gave up part of his property to widen the street. It is this unique combination that resulted in Hillside Terrace.

I wish there could have been more areas like this, but today every landowner is interested in improving their properties to increase their volume. So that is my answer to the question about Hillside

Fumihiko Maki

Terrace. It was not just my contribution, but the contribution of the client who said, "Let's make wider streets, but not allow high-density high-rises."

PH: Do you consider Hillside Terrace to be six individual projects, or one project built over many years?

FM: Neither. It was a sequence of a project in six phases.

The owner didn't have enough capital. It was actually fortunate that we had to go through six phases. Over those twenty-five years, the lifestyle in Tokyo changed drastically. Within those six phases, the housing types reflect the interests of the time—the one-room mansion, SOHO housing, small complexes, and uniform housing complexes. There is always a need for different types of housing, so there are things still waiting to be done.

RR: The opportunity of designing a slower project, such as the six phases of Hillside Terrace, is very rare in Tokyo. It is a city under constant change. Is there a period in the development of the city that was more important in your work?

FM: All of them. You see, Tokyo—as you just said—is always changing. Architects are always made to design in a certain condition, and it is interesting to work in each time under given circumstances. So, I would say all of them; I wouldn't say that any particular period has been most important.

RR: Your work has been important in developing a unique approach to the relationship between architecture and the environment. How do you describe this relationship?

FM: I don't know if you've read my essay called "Modernism on the Open Sea," in which I stressed spatialization and architecturalization. More important is socialization. I think the process of socialization can only be appreciated after observing what you have done five, ten, twenty years later.

But your question is, how do you make architectural the relationship between indoors and outdoors. It's a very important question, but it depends on the place. When we started the Aga Khan Museum in Toronto, my client, Aga Khan, gave me a five-page letter saying that in Islamic architecture the building should be sensitive to natural light. With the cold weather in Toronto, I asked to use granite, because museums there cannot have many openings to the outdoors, but in order to be very sensitive to natural light we thought we should find a white granite. That took two years, and we found one such type of granite in Brazil. We used granite because it was suitable for the given climate.

That's the kind of process I go through. My approach to architectural form always changes. I always try to find out what we should do, but again, as I mentioned at the beginning, a big building like a museum or a skyscraper requires many people to be involved. We always have group discussions, as I learned in Tange's atelier, and we make many models as we decide.

PH: How do you know where the interior ends and the exterior starts?

FM: We are interested in how we can look outside from certain places inside.

Fumihiko Maki

Hillside Terrace, Tokyo;
making space for a tree
and its shade

PH: As in the Spiral building?

FM: Yes.

PH: One moves deep within the building, up the ramp, then back toward the street in a loop. The "spiral" is this sequence of spaces, from the interior to the perimeter and back again.

FM: It was one of my early hybrid buildings. It was done in 1985. Most buildings have a singular function, but the Spiral is a complex of galleries, cafés, exhibition spaces, private clubs, offices, and so on. We thought its formal expression should also be more hybrid, but some forms from the early twentieth century are boring. So, it is a collage of different elements. Our process for arriving at a certain form is always different, never the same.

RR: How do connections to the outside change with building type?

FM: When we do low-rise buildings, I think we should be very sensitive to the immediate conditions in terms of light, appearance, and shadows. But when we do high-rise buildings, such considerations would not apply, because you become crazy if you want to make the seventh floor different from the eleventh floor, the eleventh floor from the fifteenth floor. Often, the budget requires us to have the same facade and the same attitude to the outside throughout.

RR: I would like to discuss architectural adaptability. How have your buildings adapted over time to changes?

FM: Architecture has a low criticality compared to recent technological advancements. Because of this, a building can survive over 100 years, even if social changes are occurring around it. We still have the same nature—low criticality—because a building cannot adapt to change. You can designate certain places to meet, though that also happens in houses. In the case of buildings with more social function, like museums and performing arts centers or libraries, they can adapt those buildings to social changes.

I think the same goes for our work. In Japan, when certain social requirements no longer remain, we demolish a building. In some countries they try to keep the building and use it for something different. For instance, I visited Aldo van Eyck's Amsterdam

Spiral, Tokyo; circulation
path with seating that
overlooks the street

Orphanage, built in 1960. It is a very well-known building, but there is no longer a need for an orphanage, so it has now become an office. The Dutch wanted to keep this particular form, even if it might be an obsolete type.

In Japan, if the orphanage doesn't function anymore, then they just demolish the building.

RR: The openness to demolishing gives the impression of a city that is never complete. When do you consider your own projects to be complete?

FM: When the building is given over to its society's uses, and its fate is out of our control.

Of course, some of the buildings I did in the 1960s and 1970s no longer exist, though many of them remain. Hillside Terrace will have its fifty-year anniversary this year, and the client said that if an earthquake came and it collapsed, they would build the exact building in the same way. Such clients are very rare, though.

For me, whatever I have done is always a reference to what I will do next time. We learn a lot from what we have done. For instance, children love round columns because they are reminded of hugging others. So, when we designed a facility for youth, we tried to use round columns instead of square ones.

In this case, a particular architecture becomes a means for satisfying certain behaviors. But the square column is also fine; it is just that it has its own end.

RR: Thank you very much, Maki-san.

Conversation: Itsuko Hasegawa

Rachely Rotem (RR): Let's start at the beginning. Why did you start your own architecture office?

Itsuko Hasegawa (IH): I wanted to design rather than teach at a university. When I was in high school, I studied painting—oil painting especially. I was thinking about going to art school to pursue fine arts. My mother did Japanese painting. Do you know Japanese painting?

Phu Hoang (PH): Yes.

IH: But my father was a businessman, and he was very much against me going to art school. He said that it was too free, unhealthy, and so on. I didn't know what to do. Then one day I was sitting in class, and next to me was a friend whose father happened to be an architect. I visited her in her home, and her father was there designing a house. He told me that in architecture you also paint and draw. I became interested and told my father that I would become an architect. He said, "That's OK, that would be socially valuable." So, it was in high school that I decided I was going to be an architect.

RR: Do you define your practice as designing both architecture and landscape?

IH: I consider architecture to be inclusive of everything, including the landscape.

When I was a child, my mother used to go to the field and draw pictures of wildflowers. She would take me to the field and tell me all the names of the flowers. By the time I was in middle school, I was sure that I was going to become a botanist—a doctor of plants. There was an elderly man who would take me to neighboring mountains in all seasons. He was also a botanist. He would tell me all the names of the plants.

When I started my architecture practice, I decided to incorporate research on local plants into the design process. For example, when I did this project in Niigata, I observed all the different vegetation in all seasons. I then incorporated this into the project, within the landscape that I would design.

RR: You have written about the idea of a building as a hill.

IH: Yes.

RR: How do you see the relationship between a hill and its flowers—the extra-large and extra-small scales?

IH: In architecture, there are many small things with a lot of detailed work—like designing furniture or choosing plants. It is the combination of these various things that make up architecture. This goes back to the original concept of making a forest, a field, or a sky. It is a collection of little details.

PH: Is this why mushrooms are interesting to you? They are very small organisms connected to each other to form a much larger system.

IH: The mushroom was a metaphor I used to describe traditional Japanese houses. We have traditional houses for farmers or for those involved in commerce. In areas with different climates and cultures different houses were made for each area. The microorganisms fly into the air and land in the soil, and with the unique climate and characteristics of the soil, mushrooms grow into unique beings. That's the reference I was making, to describe the way traditional houses in Japan are like mushrooms in nature.

For example, if you go to Aomori and Iwate, it's known for very deep snow in the winter. The houses there are very big because farmers do their work inside during the winter. They have big indoor spaces below deep roofs for the people to do their work.

If you go to Takayama, in central Japan, they are known for their silkworms. So, the houses are designed to harvest these silkworms. They are three stories with steep roofs. Or if you go to Okinawa, a tropical area, the floors are made with bamboo and the air can come up from the ground.

The differences are with rainfall, land, season, temperature, and materials—these are all very different, depending on the place. That's why I have described traditional Japanese architecture as akin to natural phenomena. It has developed into various forms because of these differences.

RR: On the topic of natural phenomena: When you design a project, how do you determine where the interior ends and the exterior begins?

IH: It's very difficult to say where the border between inside and outside is. In our Suzu project, we have a courtyard outside, but we've also used carpets inside that are specially made in Germany to look like natural grass, creating an outside space connected to the inside. Really, it looks like a huge Japanese field where people run around and play. For a cultural center in Niigata, a sky garden opens to the outside on the first floor.

RR: The field and garden as both exterior and interior.

IH: In the lobby of this large complex there is an extension that is a continuation of these garden bridges. The lobby inside—the architecture—and the garden outside are conceived as the same thing. They are connected.

So, it's difficult to define where the edge is—where the inside ends and the outside begins.

Itsuko Hasegawa

Fuji-Hakone-Izu National Park, Kanagawa Prefecture; mountainous area known for hot springs

RR: In your projects, architectural volumes that span open spaces also serve as infrastructure. In that sense they are both inside and outside—or an element that connects them.

IH: Yes, it is a bridge. It is a device to connect the inside and outside. But it's also a place of communication. In the cultural center in Sumida, the building had three different functions. Other architects would propose designing these different functions vertically, and people would be transported by elevator. I proposed putting three blocks on the same plane, with bridges connecting them in different ways, so that there would be various ways of networking.

PH: Is there a project of yours that you find yourself going back to as you design new projects?

IH: If we're talking about public projects, I would mention the first one I did, the Shonandai Cultural Center, as it was also my first prize for a competition. There I held discussions with local people, listening to their real voices.

RR: I have learned that you conduct many of them. Does this focus on local communities allow you to adapt to changes in society?

IH: Of course, people's lifestyles and society changes with time—people's lives also change. Even when I worked on residential houses, I thought that architecture must respond to these changes. I spent two years studying these traditional houses. What characterizes them is that inside these houses there is a void. There is basically nothing there. But you can change how you use it. For example, these sliding doors—you can put them in, or you can take them out, and if you want to use the space for a wedding you can do that. If you want to use the house for something different, you can also do that. That's how people have managed to use the same building for hundreds of years.

When I'm designing public projects, I also include a void. I think Japanese fields are voids. In my childhood, there were a lot of open fields—basically there was nothing, no public buildings or anything. Maybe some temples here and there. But we would use it differently on different occasions. For folk festivals we would put out temporary stages, and traditional performing art could be offered there, or sometimes we would make a tent and have picnics

Itsuko Hasegawa

Joshinetsu Kogen
National Park, Nagano
Prefecture; forested area
with steep cliffs

in the field. When I design public projects, I try to incorporate this concept of the field, with the hope that these buildings can be used for a long time—and actively, with a lot of joy.

RR: Do you think that with a void, you are allowing children and the elderly the ability to be freer? Since there are fewer rules about what to do in a void?

IH: A field is a place where different people can be free without being bound by its use. It is a place where there is nothing in order to realize the freedom and diversity of the place, rather than a public space that guides people's actions. I want to hear and think about the voices of people who use the space, so that I'm not just accommodating programs that have been decided upon by the municipality.

I'm very interested in this because there are actually not a lot of "lazy" people. "Lazy" is a way of describing people who are okay with just following what's already been done. Most of them are eager to learn, and to design their own ways of using a space. So, I would design the furniture, for example, but I wouldn't suggest how to arrange it. They can decide how to arrange it.

PH: Would it be true to say that the void and the hill are similar? In that people learn how to use them, and both allow for multiple ways of occupying them.

IH: It's not only the field—sometimes there are elements of water, grass, or trees. In all of this, I make very minimal interventions. The field is left open for users to use it in different ways. They can decide to use it as a place to lie down; it can be a meeting place for a book club; it can be a place for children to play.

There is a wind tower in the Shonandai Cultural Center and it makes the movement of the wind visible. I explain to children about the cloud and light changes. There is also *suikinkutsu*, a special technique of gardening. It's a sound installation that we create in gardens. There's a ceramic vase that is buried, and there are different ways of letting the water drop so that you hear the echoes of the water. There are many gardens in Kyoto that have *suikinkutsu*. The vase amplifies the water's sound.

RR: Interesting. You work with ground and water to control sound.

IH: But they are also hidden in the ground.

RR: When you are designing, how do you know a project is complete?

IH: I actually visit projects for many years after they are realized. For the Shonandai Cultural Center, I commuted there for more than ten years. I always want to make sure that people are using them, and that exchanges we had during the design process are happening. So, until I see that people are realizing what we discussed in our sessions, I don't feel that a project is complete.

I programmed various workshops where I continued to have exchanges with children. We would do workshops about designing a house, drawing a city together, or talking about different histories. Over the years, we have many programs that take place in the projects. I observe how people are using the space. I visit them to make sure they are being used in the ways we've discussed.

RR: We will end here on the topic of incompletion. This has been very interesting. *Arigatou gozaimasu.*

IH: *Arigatou gozaimasu.*

Conversation:
Kengo Kuma

Rachely Rotem (RR): Let's start at the beginning: Why did you start your own architecture practice?

Kengo Kuma (KK): I think it was necessary to realize my philosophy. And I didn't want to work for other people! (Laughter)

RR: On this topic of beginnings, how do you start designing a project?

KK: I like to walk a site by myself, by foot. Without this kind of direct experience, I cannot start designing. Sometimes clients send me videos and images of a site and say, "Please start the project right away!" But I don't like to do projects that way. It is too indirect. Video is insufficient—it's not enough to get started.

I like to get a sense of the wind of the site, the life of the site, and know its surroundings. This is very important. Our first step is always to go to the site, and the second step is to make a physical model including its surroundings. Physical models can teach me many things about a place.

Phu Hoang (PH): What do you learn from models?

KK: We have team meetings with the model in the center of the table. Without physical models, the team discussion cannot capture the reality of a place. The conversation turns to abstractions, and I don't like that kind of abstract conversation. We make many, many models.

RR: You have described in your writing that architecture is a mediator between oneself and nature.

KK: Yes, I think it is a kind of mediator. I want it to be a mediator between the site and humans. A mediator has a very important role, as it can pick up on the essence of a place. To be a mediator is a kind of a challenge. Some architects ignore a place and just repeat their own style. I don't want to do that.

RR: If architecture is a mediator between a site and people, does this result in material thinness?

KK: Thinness creates the flow of a place. I want to create a flow of wind and light, and a flow of humans. If you do not do that, then there is a solid block that refuses that flow. I always want to make things as thin as possible.

PH: In your Nezu Museum—especially the detail of the roof—you set back the edge so that the expression of the roof is extremely thin.

KK: It's also related to flow. Every element of the space should be very sensitive and delicate. That is my goal with design.

PH: You are speaking about layers—layers between a roof exterior and its interior.

KK: Yes.

RR: Perhaps we should also discuss nature, since that is what architecture mediates. What is nature for you?

KK: Nature is all our surroundings. The addition of a building in a city adds nature to a place. I often get the question: What is the difference between building in nature and building in the city? I think both are in nature. In the city, we also have the wind and the light—there really is no difference.

RR: You wrote in *Anti-Object* about the ideal city as particles, a degrading of wilderness. We see this in Tokyo, with its extra-small pixels of residential buildings. How do you see these extreme scales at work in a large metropolis?

KK: I'm very sensitive to the size of pixels in the city, but there are many layers of pixels. The building itself is large, but the size of the curtain wall is another size, another layer of scale. And I consider everything—not only the size of the building. The building skin also has a scale. And for every place, these different scales exist.

And in that kind of chaos, we design something. But the chaos is not just chaos; the chaos also has some layers. I want to feel something from this chaos, and then I want to reflect it.

RR: Is this chaos both literal and perceptual?

KK: Yes, I think so. I have been greatly influenced by the theory of affordances. Do you know it?

James Gibson studied the theory in the 1940s. His understanding of the environment was that it consists of pixels, and life—even animals—comes from the pixel. If pixels don't exist, animals cannot find their position. This is why a simple white cube is not a good atmosphere for an animal.

PH: Tokyo is a city under constant change. Which period of practicing in Tokyo has been most instrumental?

KK: The 1990s was a very critical time in Tokyo. Before the 1990s, Tokyo was always trying to follow modernist design. In the 1990s, the economy was very bad, and there were no new projects. I couldn't find a project in Tokyo. So, I went to the countryside to do small projects.

Even now, I especially like to work for small rural communities—but not only in Japan. For example, I'm working in a small community in Turkey. I am designing a small building for them. In those kinds of small communities, the role of architecture is bigger than it is in the big city.

Now back to the 1990s: most Japanese architects began to think that we should find our own way. The country's economic expansion had ended, and we could not catch up with globalization. There started to be a feeling of finding our own way. We faced our own reality—for instance, our reality of a society with fewer kids, and an aging society.

Nezu Museum, Tokyo; roof line on exterior is followed on the interior

PH: So, the economic crisis—when you started your practice—allowed some architects to look inward and create their own voice that now has a global identity.

KK: Yes. For me it was a very, very important period. I was able to find my own voice in that period. The voice I established then was recognized in other countries, and that is when I began to work abroad.

RR: Is there a project of yours that you find yourself returning to as you work on new projects?

KK: The Hiroshige Museum, completed in 2000, was an early project where I used wood as a screen. With the Hiroshige Museum, I had the idea to use it for every part of the building. I repeated the screen—the same detail for the ceiling, the roof, and the vertical screen—using the same louvers. I was happy to have found that method.

PH: Which we see also, for example, in the Suntory Museum in Tokyo.

KK: Yes, the Suntory Museum came after Hiroshige.
 The Bamboo House in China was also a very important project. It was completed in 2002 or 2003. But the basic method of the Bamboo House came from Hiroshige.

RR: When you work on a project, when do you know the design is complete?

KK: At some point, after some days, I know the project is done. Sometimes, from the very beginning, I have a very strong idea for every detail of the planning. But mostly it's between the design phase and some days later when I say, "Ah, it's done."

RR: And in terms of physical "completion," where does the interior of a building end and its exterior begin?

KK: For us, indoor and outdoor does not matter so much. Some consistent ideas cover the interior and exterior. We always try to find that kind of consistent, strong idea. For example, Hiroshige's louvers cover both the exterior and the interior.

RR: So, you treat the exterior and interior the same?

KK: Yes. For some projects—for example, a big hotel—we work with an interior designer, and the interior and exterior should be totally separate. I don't like that kind of method or process. I want to cover everything with the same idea.

PH: Returning to the Hiroshige Museum: What is the role of louver on the exterior and interior?

KK: The basic idea for a louver screen is to create a shadow. A screen is a screen of light, a screen of wind. And with the light that comes from one direction, we can create shadows behind that. Glass cannot create shadows. I'm not satisfied with glass.

I want to have a screen to control the space, to create shadows. For life—humans and animals—the shadow is very important. A shadow can give a sense of protection, and a sense of healing. Humans started living in the forest because the forest had many shadows. Life started in the forest.

RR: These building elements—the thin edge of a roof and the louver screen—are they designed to connect us to the site's ground?

KK: Yes.

RR: So, the ground is the most important building element?

KK: Yes, but the ground is also related to Gibson's ideas. The ground has many messages about life. Even for the pilot in the sky—and Gibson used to be a pilot—the pilot finds a vertical ground in the sky. They can find the distance and the target, all based on the vertical ground in the sky.

Life needs a ground. Especially for the traditional Japanese building, we use the ground as the most important design element. For instance, the tatami mat; compared to the ground and the floors, the vertical elements like walls are not so necessary. I like this method very much.

PH: I am reminded of your writing about emptiness—for example, the open-air theater. How do you design for emptiness?

KK: There are many scales of emptiness. Between particles there is emptiness, and in big volumes of buildings we also try to cut the emptiness. In the Hiroshige Museum, we cut the building to create emptiness, to cover the emptiness. We have a big roof, but in the center, we have empty space.

I have repeated this method for many projects. In a recent project, the V&A Museum, we cut the building to have empty space that connects the river and the city. This is emptiness between the volumes. But there have also been projects where we have emptiness between the vertical and horizontal louvers.

RR: Is this emptiness space for the public?

KK: Yes, the emptiness is for the public, and the emptiness also brings nature to us.

RR: I like that very much.

PH: Did your interest in particles begin with digital technologies?

KK: Yes. I myself am very much influenced by digital technology. You both came from Columbia University and teach there?

PH: Yes.

KK: I also studied at Columbia, in 1986. At that time, Bernard Tschumi came to Columbia and started the paperless studios, and my friends Stan Allen, Hani Rashid, and Greg Lynn were all at Columbia. I was looking at what they were doing, and they used digital technology basically to create organic forms. I didn't like that kind of approach. It reminds me of a kind of modernist design in the 1920s.

You know Mario Carpo? He's the author of *The Alphabet and the Algorithm*?

He also wrote a book about the second digital era. The first digital era was the 1990s. The aim of that generation's design was to create that new kind of form. In the second digital era, the goal is different. He also picks up on my design as part of the second era. He says that most people think that Kuma-san's design is not really digital. Actually, this way of gathering small units to create a kind of cloud is typical of second-generation digital.

Actually, to use those small units for a building requires a digital simulation. Most of our staff uses Grasshopper, and sometimes we use CATIA. It repeats the pitch of the unit, the size of the unit, and that data is transferred to a structural engineer. Our design process is that kind of back and forth between the engineers and us. We change the simulation a little bit and it affects the structure.

I doubted digital design in the 1990s, but finally, after 2000, I'm unconsciously going in that direction. Not from the beginning, and not in the same way as the first generation.

RR: You are allowing the extra-small scale to become larger.

KK: Yes. Basically, I'm not interested in the silhouette of the building. In the twentieth century, architects started designing from the silhouette of the building. The silhouette was first. How to create the monumental silhouette was the most important thing in the twentieth century. My method is the opposite. Start from the small unit—and how to gather this small unit—and eventually you can find the structure.

RR: Thank you very much. We especially appreciate it, as it is so early in the morning.

KK: Actually, I just flew back from New York last night at midnight!

Conversation: Ryue Nishizawa

Phu Hoang (PH): Let's start at the beginning: Why did you decide to start your architecture practice?

Ryue Nishizawa (RN): Why?

PH: Yes, why?

RN: Just because everybody around me did! It's not a great reason. All architecture students dream of becoming architects someday—whether at a big firm or in a small organization. I don't know how young people think now, but students in Japan were like that in the 1980s and 1990s.

PH: Important architecture practices came out of that time period.

RN: Yes. I had joined Sejima-san's office and, after working there for five years, I decided to become an independent architect. Sejima-san and I discussed creating a new form of collaboration, working mainly on international projects.

In those days, Japan was in a depressed economic period. We didn't have any public competitions in Japan, so many architects tried to go abroad to get work. Those were the days when Europe was becoming more integrated and created the Eurozone. They started organizing public competitions, open not only to local but also to international architects.

PH: Also, on this topic of beginnings: When you start a project, how do you start designing?

RN: In the first meeting, I don't always understand everything the client wants. On the site, I don't immediately see all of the context. So, we spend a long time at the beginning of design. This is the period when we learn what the client's principles are, or what the site's potential context is. This is our first step—program and site.

PH: Has there been a particular period in Tokyo's history that has been instrumental to your practice?

RN: I was born in Tokyo and I grew up there. I don't know any other city besides Tokyo.

I realized at some point that Tokyo is not normal. When I went to Europe, I saw that all other cities are not like Tokyo. This experience of Europe was important to me. I was able to look back at myself and at Tokyo.

PH: So, it took going outside of Tokyo to see it?

RN: Yes—or Japan. When I was working in Tokyo in the early 1990s, nobody talked about "Tokyo," "Japan." Because there were no international people here, we didn't talk about Tokyo. If you go to

Ryue Nishizawa

Moriyama House, Tokyo;
semi-exterior circulation
connects small structures

India, there is no "Indian curry" there, because everything is an Indian curry. So here, in those days, "Japan," "Tokyo"—these were words we never used. But when I went to Europe . . .

PH: When was that?

RN: I first went in 1993. Those days, people around me in Europe would say, "Japan, Japan, Japan. You are very Japanese." And at first I felt a little uncomfortable, because I had never been told, "You are really Japanese." But in Europe I found that Japan was a concept, Tokyo was a concept.

PH: So, you were able to see Japanese architecture in a way that you couldn't when you were within it?

RN: Maybe I had a new point of view when I was outside Japan. When you are inside, you don't see it. But when you go outside, you do.

PH: On this topic of been inside and outside: What is the relationship between the extra-small scale in your work and the very large urban scale?

RN: I am not sure what kind of relationship it is, but there are a few aspects of architecture that I'm interested in, that I love.

One of them is that architecture can create a place. If you create architecture, it creates a meeting place under the roof, even if there is no program. Architecture suggests that there is a place there.

Another issue that I am interested in is that architecture doesn't belong to humans.

Ryue Nishizawa

PH: Who does it belong to?

RN: Architecture doesn't belong to anyone.

When we design, we think about architecture for people, and we imagine how to use it.

But after it is made, it is released into the world. Even if I have a scenario in mind of how it will be used, people use it in a really different way—different from what I expected. Architecture always comes with this overexpectation.

It also remains for thousands of years. These days, programs change, people change, nations change—everything changes, but still architecture remains. So, I can't say architecture always belong to us.

PH: Are you saying that architecture is never truly completed? Maybe in terms of the building process, but it's not completed in the world.

RN: It never belongs to anybody; it never belongs to anything. Everybody has a right to access it. It's more like nature.

PH: Architecture for everyone.

RN: When I did a house for a friend, Moriyama House, I thought that I had made it. But when Moriyama-san invited his friend over, he said, "Look, I made it." And when my friend, who was the contractor, also invited his friend, *he* said, "I made it." Everybody said, "I made it."

Architecture is social. Everybody can say "I made it." I think this process becomes real life. But on the other hand, architecture is independent. It becomes free. It becomes independent from us.

PH: It is more open?

RN: Yes, more open.

PH: Is there a project of yours that you find yourself returning to when you design new projects?

RN: A project is a way for me to think about an issue. For instance, openness is an issue that I've spent more than twenty years thinking about. It's not an issue that only one project could finalize.

When we find an important issue, it suggests that there will be many projects responding to it. Some projects create issues, and then invite new projects.

PH: So, you don't return to any projects, but you return to the issues that come from projects.

RN: Yes. In other words, it's a history. But this history only happens within my work. One project invites a new project. The new project invites a *new*, new project. This continuity is very important.

PH: With the issue of openness, where do you draw the line between where the inside ends and the outside begins?

RN: The boundary is a very Western issue. Since Europe is very cold, they needed to create walls. China is like an endless world, so they created borders to define their cities. There people define a city by a wall in the desert.

In Japan, there is no concept of the border. We have oceans and mountains. Ninety percent of our land is occupied by mountains. There is very little space for architecture here. So, the border is already defined. There are other reasons why we have no borders. For example, there is the diversity of the climate.

Ryue Nishizawa

PH: How does climate produce fewer borders?

RN: People don't like humidity. The ground is really wet. That's why traditional Japanese architecture has the floor raised and walls open. With humidity, if you create walls around you, you will suffer. You need to open walls to feel comfortable.

I'm really influenced by traditional Japanese architecture. I don't know what I have done to develop it further, but everything we do is traditional. What is new? That I don't know. Maybe nothing! It is repetition of the traditional, but we live in a different time.

PH: But in your work you open up borders even more, such as in the Teshima Art Museum.

RN: In the Teshima Art Museum, I decided to use a free curve. There are many reasons for this. One is that when people stay inside, they still feel the outside. They still feel nature.

If I did straight walls, you would feel as if you were in a box. I would have had to cut the mountain next to the museum. With a free curve, I didn't have to cut it since I designed around it.

When the mountain comes in, architecture sets back. When the mountain sets back, architecture can go in. The relationship to nature is not about how big to make a window. It is not only visual. It is situational and the context is important.

The border is an interesting issue that Japanese architecture has been trying to contend with. European architecture creates walls to define the inside and outside, but Japanese architecture has so many layers within it. Like the roof, the *engawa*, or the garden around it. It is like a person wearing many clothes. Between inside and outside there are many in-between spaces.

PH: True. Despite the transparency of glass, European modernism created more borders.

RN: Yes. That's impressive. They are very strong people. I'm really amazed by their ways. But I understand that we can never do this because it's a different culture.

In Japan, everybody experiences space gradually—from outside to inside gradually. Everybody experiences it as a kind of continuity. A collection of in-between spaces brings you from the outside to the inside.

PH: I would like to discuss incompletion. You wrote in the introduction to your small book *Studies* that you like the debris of study models, because they are incomplete.

RN: If we had time, a study would go on forever. But fortunately, we have deadlines! That's how they become temporarily complete.

PH: So, it's project deadlines that makes completion?

RN: If there were no deadlines, it would never be completed. I always think about painters. The process of creating a painting has no end, because you can paint it and you can paint over it. With a sculpture, if you keep on sculpting, at some point it becomes nothing.

But a painting you can do forever. It's the same with architecture.

PH: You are speaking about incompleteness in terms of time, specifically with the design process. Is there physical incompleteness?

RN: Le Corbusier's work was not always completed. For instance, with Unité d'Habitation or La Tourette, his method was addition, adding something on. It's his way of saying there is no end, that there is no big picture. One plus one, plus one, plus one . . .

In Japan we start by dividing. The big picture never changes. But Le Corbusier adds. It's growing. Even after its completion, I feel that it's still growing.

PH: If Le Corbusier is about addition, your architecture is about division?

RN: Or reduction. Make it simple. Le Corbusier was really complex. I think he was a great architect.

PH: Last question, which is also about the incomplete: Can architecture adapt to future changes in society?

RN: This is a difficult question. The museum is becoming something more than a museum. Before, the museum was a place where people learned about art. Now, the museum has more programs. I feel that the museum is changing.

When we did the Rolex Learning Center, in Lausanne, I went to Columbia University to see the business school. When there was a ten-minute break between classes, students moved from one classroom to another and asked the teacher questions that they couldn't ask during class. This often happened in the corridor.

I realized that the corridor was a place where people learned and studied. And then the school started putting furniture in the corridor to hold different types of discussions. What I learned was that students study everywhere. Not only in class, but also in the corridor, even outside. This became an important concept in the Rolex Learning Center.

PH: You are suggesting that the boundaries of program change as society changes.

RN: I think that's a really great idea. When architecture becomes new, the program also becomes new. Also, the mode of discussion becomes new. This is why in Lausanne we made a landscape inside architecture.

PH: Thank you very much, Nishizawa-san. This has been a fascinating conversation.

RN: Thank you very much.

Hiroshi Senju Museum, Karuizawa; interior floor follows the exterior ground

Conversation:
Takaharu and Yui Tezuka

Phu Hoang (PH): Let's start at the beginning: Why did you both start your architecture practice?

Yui Tezuka (YT): My father was an architect and I was born in the house that he designed. I loved that house very much, so when I was twelve, I decided to become an architect and then went to university.

Takaharu Tezuka (TT): Actually, both of us are children of architects. My father was also an architect, so I was always surrounded by architecture books. There used to be a magazine called *SD* (*Space Design*), and he was one of its founders.

While I was in school, my professor asked me, "Do you want to work in the United States?" I said, "No, no." Then he asked, "Are you looking at Europe? Why not look there? Richard Rogers's office is very good. Though you may go bankrupt."

I found Richard Rogers's office offered a lot of freedom, which I liked. At the time, Yui was an undergraduate student in Japan. Two years after I started working for Richard Rogers, we got married, she came to London, and she went to study at The Bartlett. That's where Yui met Ron Herron and Peter Cook.

But we were not sure if we should start an office. One day, one of my uncles called—it's a typical story, your relatives are the first ones to give you a project. My uncle called my father: "I want your son to design my hospital." But my father said, "No, he's not ready. I can do it for you." So, he had his office prepare to design the project. One day, I called my father and he said, "By the way, your uncle called, and he wanted you to design a hospital, but I said you're not ready yet." "What?" I said. "No, no, it's my project, you're supposed to give it to me!"

He told me, "You're not ready." I said, "No, I'll show you," and the next day I took a flight back to Tokyo and tried to convince him. He said, "No, you are still young; you are still just in training." I said, "I'm ready because I've gained a lot of experience. I'm in charge of Heathrow's Terminal 5." Then my father said, "OK, I'll give you from now until tomorrow morning. It's almost midnight. If you can finish your presentation within six hours, I'll take you to your uncle, and if you make a presentation that he's impressed with, you can do the work." When I went to present it to my uncle, he said, "Oh, this is a very good project, but we already have a design. Thank you—if you had called me earlier, then I would have asked you to do the job."

A few months later, my uncle called me directly. He said, "We asked your father's company to design my hospital, but their budget has doubled. It was supposed to be eight million dollars; it has become sixteen million dollars. Can you make it for eight million dollars?" I said, "No problem."

I went to Richard and told him, "One of my uncles called and he wants me to design a hospital, but if you want me to stay, I can stay for you." I was expecting him to say please stay, but he said, "No, you can go." There is one rule in my office: if somebody wants to start their own business, I will always let the person go.

I went back and got my first project built. That project won the Minister's Prize and then our university—where I teach now—called me and said, "Do you want to be professor?" So, I became professor and that is how I started my practice. And four years later we had a drink with Richard Rogers and the nicest comment I got from Richard was, "Have you gone bankrupt yet?" That is the story of how we started.

Rachely Rotem (RR): Has there been a particular period in Tokyo that was an important moment—or a turning point—for your practice?

TT: People have asked me before when our turning point was, but I am always getting turned around. I am always bumping into dead ends and going back and forth. And wherever I go, an economic crisis seems to happen. When we went to the United States, the economy collapsed, and then I went to London and the economy collapsed, and when I came back to Japan the economy collapsed. So, we only know bad economic moments.

PH: Have these economic recessions been important to the development of your practice?

TT: Yes they were, because we are survivors. The practice can live with small projects. We started with an eight-million-dollar project—a hospital—and then went to a very small scale, a 100-square-meter house project. Our office does both large- and small-scale projects. Usually with offices like this—we have thirty people—they don't take on small projects. But we think that it is very important to do small projects, because it's the only way to teach young architects a different way to practice. Also, houses are very basic. The biggest project we're doing is 170,000 square meters; the smallest is eighty square meters, but both are very important. So, I would say that there has been no turning point for us.

PH: How do you start designing a project?

TT: We make many, many models—we make at least fifty models to get our ideas. We do not start from sketches, and I even make models by myself—for the initial models this is very important. A handmade model is the only way to start designing. Nowadays, students think about starting with 3-D modeling. I don't do that. 3-D modeling is a good way to confirm a project, but I don't think it's a good beginning.

Takaharu and Yui Tezuka

Fuji Kindergarten, Tokyo;
a large roof doubles as an
open play area for children

PH: Tokyo's residential neighborhoods are comprised of many micro-sized buildings—with an average lot size of 750 square feet. The contrast between this diminutive scale with the city's vastness—over thirty-six million people—is remarkable.

TT: Yes, I think that Tokyo is a peculiar city in a peculiar situation. In the center of Tokyo, you have high-rises along the big streets, but once you walk past the streets you have small houses. Some people say that is bad, some people say it's good, and I used to say it's just not efficient. Now, I find that it's a unique feature of Tokyo because you can maintain diversity. There are some completely outdated areas, but those are juxtaposed within many layers of the city.

In Japan, people must build a house before they're forty years old because in terms of real estate value, all of it is in the land. When you buy a property, there usually is not a house on it and you must build one. But to do that you need to get a loan from the bank, and it takes about twenty, thirty, or even forty years to pay it back. It's very different from the United States, where, if you buy something, you may be able to sell it for more money a few years later. In Japan, this doesn't happen. If you buy a house for half a million dollars, it could be worth just a quarter million dollars years later, though you must keep paying the loan. So, once you buy a house it's for a lifetime.

PH: Part of this idea of scale is the border between architecture and the environment. How do you design for where the inside ends and the outside begins?

TT: There is no boundary. Everything is part of the whole. It's a very Asian point of view. In European thinking, architecture is defined as a shelter for protecting people. But it's more important to breathe than to have shelter. I think you might know a sketch by Jørn Utzon: he designed a Japanese house with just a roof and no walls. He didn't consider it to be architecture without walls; a building with walls is architecture. For him, walls were very important. We did a project called Engawa House.

PH: I know it. It is a house that is open to its neighbors. It is domestic and urban at the same time.

TT: It is not a house with a porch. The house itself is a porch. If we're talking about a boundary, maybe the only boundary is a person's skin.

We have a recording from when we were in Bali. When we returned to Japan and listened to it, we heard for the first time the background noise of insects. When we were there, we did not hear the noise because it was canceled by our brains. Our brains are a noise-canceling system. Our bodies are the same. When you are part of a whole existence, you can cancel out the noise. When you are in the jungle, you can cancel whatever you feel is not necessary. But once you become disconnected from the environment, your system starts going wrong.

Children are the same way. Researchers now suspect that many symptoms of autism are caused by exactly this: children listening to their own body's noise. A baby sleeps quite well in a noisy restaurant, but in a quiet room they start to cry. And we also know that newborn babies need to be in a noisy place, and when they're put in a quiet space with special care they start having problems.

Many things suggest we shouldn't be too independent. We are a part of a whole of existence. When we designed a hospital for an infertility clinic, we did some research about the immune system. Many women are having problems with infertility because they were kept in a clean environment. We designed a hospital so that they can be in more natural conditions. When you have treatment like surgery, of course they have to be in a clean environment. But after treatment, they need to be in a normal environment. We are symbiotic—the quantity of bacteria we have in our bodies is more than the number of cells in our bodies. We need to maintain this kind of equilibrium in the hospital.

We need to have balance. When you're put into a clean environment, the immune system starts attacking its own body and killing embryos. When we designed this hospital, we made everything open. Whatever we design is based on this kind of thinking: How can we breathe within our external environment?

RR: You are describing a different way to think about nature—it is not outside of our bodies or even our buildings, but it is an interdependent part of ourselves.

TT: Oh, there are many ways to talk about nature. I once had a discussion with Dominique Perrault. We were talking about the difference between nature and the natural.

The "natural" is a redefinition of nature. The natural is processed by people. For humans, this has been necessary. But "nature" is as it is, with people as a part of it. Instead of changing the environment, we need to find a way to live with it.

PH: I have a last question, which is coincidentally about endings. How do you know when a project is complete?

TT: The end of construction is always the beginning.

YT: Before people start using it, architecture is just any ordinary thing, but once people come in, it becomes alive. It starts to breathe. I like those kinds of moments. I think that is the start of architecture and not it's end.

TT: There is no end to a project. Maybe "complete" is when a building is demolished. The thing is, except for our temporary structures, none of our buildings have been destroyed. We have built more than 180 projects.

Takaharu and Yui Tezuka

Fuji Kindergarten, Tokyo; a central open area surrounded by trees growing through the large roof

PH: So, you haven't completed anything?

TT: No! (Laughter)

PH: Architecture as the means but not the end.

TT: Yes, it is a beginning. Architecture is not a thing but an event. And things go on.

RR: So, you started your practice with Soejima Hospital for the elderly. With Fuji Kindergarten, you were designing for young children. You have designed toward the beginning and end of life.

TT: It's all the same.

RR: You treat them the same?

YT: We always try to think about who is using the building itself. The difficult thing is that when we design a hospital, the patient is not at the meeting. So, we have to be in the role of the patient. (Laughter)

TT: I used to tell the owner of Fuji Kindergarten: I'm a surfboard maker. I know what's good for you, but you must be a good surfer. He's a good surfer, in fact he surfs very well. But without my surfboard, he can't surf.

TT: It's very important to design for many generations. When you design a playground to be used only by kids, it becomes just a tool for play. Usually, kids will get bored because it's not real. A tool for play is a symbol for their life. And when you use such a tool, it always comes with instructions: what you're not supposed to do. But if you go into a nice town, it can be improvised in many ways.
　　It was interesting when we went to Casa Milà, designed by Gaudí, and experienced its roof. The angles of the roof with people moving up and down it—our son was very small, but he really loved it. And grown-ups like it too, because they never get bored. My point is,

when you make something real, you don't need to wake up, but when you try to make something a dream, you will wake up. We want to build something real yet interesting.

RR: What we define as "real" seems to be increasingly in question these days.

TT: Yes, but "real" doesn't mean to be boring. Sometimes you can find the real very interesting. It is reality.

RR: Tomorrow we are going to see one of your realities.

TT: Which one?

RR: Fuji Kindergarten.

TT: Ah, yes. You should talk to the owner. He's a very, very interesting guy. I told you the story: I'm the surfboard maker, he's a surfboarder. (Laughter)

Conversation:
Go Hasegawa

Phu Hoang (PH): Let's start at the beginning: Why did you start your own architecture practice?

Go Hasegawa (GH): Maybe it was my father's influence. My father is a ship engineer for big ships. He doesn't design them; he's a mechanical engineer, so he plans the ship turbines and engines.

When I was a kid, every weekend he would draw ships at the dining table. So, I was very used to these kinds of drawings and their tools. I absorbed this sense of scale unconsciously because he took me several times to the ceremonies when a ship enters the ocean. I was so surprised to see that some of the ships were 300 meters long!

PH: Given your early experiences with extreme scales, how has it influenced your architecture?

GH: A ship is bigger than a building, but I was so surprised by the concept of scale—from drawings on A1-sized paper to a 300-meter ship. This was perhaps a foundational experience in my life.

When I was in high school, I had to choose my course of study for university and architecture sounded the most exciting of all the offerings. It was around then that I saw the monograph of Kazuo Shinohara. He was teaching at Tokyo Tech, where I would eventually study. He was one of my early influences.

PH: How do you start to design a project?

GH: I think it's very simple. For me, the place and person—meaning the context of the site and client—are very important. We really focus on each client's characteristics and emphasize the potential of the project on the human level. Sometimes, when I lecture in certain places in the US, American architects say, "Your approach is too specific to the human. Architecture should be more general." That is the reaction to my work in the States. As you know, I do very low or very high ceiling heights, and that is unacceptable to them.

PH: The standardization of scale is part of modernism or perhaps a universal quality of space—this has become integral to US building standards.

GH: "This is too low, Go. It's not good for the human scale." But I think that there is a very important phenomenon in my generation of architects. Of course, we try to reinvent the concept and potential of architecture, but we also try to investigate a sort of human potential at the same time. We believe that we can find something new from the characteristics of each person—an idea of the space of architecture that also works for other people. It is not for everybody. But, for example, my Kyodo House—which has a roof shade and a very low ceiling on the ground floor—is very specific because it's a house for an editor who has a lot of books and no kids. It's a very small house. I believe that if ten people want to live there in the world, then that is fine.

Go Hasegawa

Tokyo is a city of extreme scales, from the extra small to the extremely large

PH: You are speaking of the need for the specific to overcome the generic.

GH: Yes. We architects believe in the twentieth century idea of the universality of architecture too much. Architecture does not need to be accepted by everybody, right? For example, universal space as conceived by Mies van der Rohe was successful. But it's everywhere now.

I would say that it's not necessary for it to be accepted by all humans. Instead, we should listen to the characteristic of the space: whether there's a garden in front of the building or not, or what kind of building it is, and its surrounding situation. At the same time, each person is very different. I have never seen the same character in any of my ex-clients. Every client is different.

PH: Is designing for the character of each client part of your idea about designing architecture for people?

GH: This is why US architects are not interesting to me. To me, they are just playing formal games. We can come closer to people.

Hirata, Ishigami, Nakayama—some interesting architects of my generation are also focusing on this idea. Of course, our styles and designs are totally different, but I believe there is some similarity in our interests. I would say that we are all interested in humans.

PH: How would you characterize the human experience of extremely different scales in Tokyo—specifically, between very small houses and the mega-scale urbanism?

GH: I think that is the most interesting characteristic of Tokyo. For example, on the west side of Shinjuku, next to a tall tower, there are many two-story houses. I really like this situation because they are the same building. The tower and the tiny houses are kind of similar—kind of the same and kind of equal. They share the ground and the neighborhood, and their only difference is in size and height. There is a kind of unconscious similarity in Tokyo because it is a city without clear divisions between residential and high-rise areas.

We all share the same ground. This is why I always focus on typology: for example, the residential house. The Kyodo House is a four-story apartment. It's a kind of ambiguous neighborhood, but relatively speaking there are a lot of two-story houses around it. So,

Go Hasegawa

I started from this common type in the neighborhood while at the same time I believed in a sort of independence from the surrounding area. My idea is contradictory: I want my building to be connected to its surroundings, but, on the other hand, I want it to be independent.

PH: You've written about this similarity as being simultaneously connected but independent.

GH: Yes.

PH: Your idea is that scale is not only an architectural metric, but it also guides human experience. What is the scale that you find most capable of "being connected but independent"?

GH: Yes, scale and proportion are very important. I'd say those two things are almost everything in my process.

I don't deny the comfort of the human scale, but I also believe that we can propose a new type of human scale because our sense of it is always changing. For example, I am currently connected to the opposite side of the river [gestures to river across the main road], but my sense is also shifting between the nearby scale of this tower [gestures to tower]. These various types of scale are always part of Tokyo's character. That's why I like the gaps between buildings. It's a very human scale, as narrow as one meter wide, but at the same time, as tall as a building—at the building scale.

I want to shift or expand the concept of human scale in a more natural way as we experience it. In the twentieth century, scale was divided from the furniture scale to the room scale, from the building scale to the urban scale. But our lives are not like that. The answer to your question is that I would like to create ambiguity among various types of scale. I combine various types of scale within one space. So, even if you're in a small house, you can feel its tiny scale at the same time as you feel the city scale. When I talk about the common ground of the residential house and the tower, it's not just a metaphor, but my honest feeling about living in Tokyo. This is an important basis for my practice.

PH: You have mentioned your Kyodo House a couple times—is this a project that you find yourself returning to as you design new projects?

GH: Maybe other projects have shown my intentions more clearly, like the Kyodo House and Pilotis in a Forest, so they're useful for explaining my ideas. But it doesn't mean that they're better than any other projects. Every project is connected.

PH: Continuing about scale, where does the inside end and the outside begin?

GH: They're not separated at all. This is a very Japanese idea, like the sliding shoji screen. It is all very flexible, and we don't think of the inside as architecture and the outside as the city. It's totally connected; we are part of nature. It's the same as the various types of scales I've been talking about. For me, the sense of scale and the concepts of inside and outside are totally connected.

PH: You mentioned the word "nature." How would you define nature?

GH: What is nature? Maybe people define architecture in contrast to nature, but for me architecture is also nature. That is not because there are plants in it. Plants are just symbols of nature.

The condition of light is already nature; something that connects to the environment is already nature. I don't use the word "nature" as much as the word "environment."

PH: What is the difference between environment and nature?

GH: The environment has no boundaries. People believe that nature is the countryside or the tree and so on, but with the environment we can deal equally with the interior and exterior. I don't use the word "nature" so much because "environment" can traverse the inside boundary made by the building. I've never thought about this before, but it's important.

PH: The House in Gotanda brings the inside out, bringing domestic activities to the outside, while in Nerima Apartments the outside is brought in. When do you design for inside-out versus outside-in?

GH: It depends on the situation. In the center of Tokyo, as in the Nerima Apartments, I found it was necessary to make a space that was a little bit protected from its surroundings. So, an outdoor space that's like a room is appropriate for those who live there. Whether inside-out or outside-in depends on the surroundings as well as whether it's comfortable for people. Take the pilotis space in Pilotis in a Forest. It's an outside space that's like an inside. Here, the challenge was making a space for people to stay outside as long as possible.

That was a challenge of my own because the weekend house is always a symbol of rich people who want to stay inside. Even if it will take them three hours to get back home, they stay inside and watch the trees from within. It's a pity. It's a challenge to make comfortable outside spaces that are almost like an inside.

PH: Yes, it is—regardless of the site, it is about understanding the invisible character of an environment.

GH: Yes. And it also depends on the client's character.

PH: There are two ways in which you have discussed the incomplete temporal and spatial character of architecture. One is that you continue to build models even while a project is in construction. The second is that it is not possible to fully enclose interior space.

GH: What is the relationship between them? My feeling may be closer to the first example. I never talk about the completion of a project. Even now, my first building is not completed. If I can learn something from that project, it's still not completed. We continue to learn from our experience. And if I finish the design process, we can learn and, if possible, make changes during construction. Or even after the completion of the building itself, I can notice things when I visit the building and see how it behaves and learn from what it says to me.

PH: What about designing fully enclosed interiors?

GH: For me, interior design is difficult because it is impossible to think only of the inside. And it's not interesting to limit the territory of architects. Even if it is, I've never done it, and I have no experience with interior design. But if I did, I believe that I would want to overcome the various types of gaps, like inside and outside, artificial and natural, and so on.

Go Hasegawa

Gaps between Tokyo's buildings for fire separation are also outdoor microclimates

PH: On a different topic, you have written that history is continuous and open-ended. Given Japan's changing society, how can architecture define places within this continuum?

GH: I don't believe in dealing with society as a tool of design. I don't deny that society exists, and I totally believe that every building is a social thing—even the tiniest house. Yet it's not simply a product of today's society. And that's why I don't use the word "society" when I write about my projects. I am strongly influenced by society today, but at the same time I want to be free from it. Or I believe in a sort of autonomy of architecture, and I want to make buildings that can also produce reactions from people in the next century. For me, that is architecture. Beyond different societies or contexts, we can communicate with each other.

PH: In fact, you are thinking about the future when you speak about history.

GH: Yes. I did an exhibition with Kersten Geers and David van Severen at the Canadian Centre for Architecture called *Beside History*. It was a very important experience for me, in which I totally understood again who I am. I never thought about architectural generations, and I don't like to discuss them so much, but my sense of history is totally different from older generations. We—Kersten, David, and I—were all born around the same year. I was born in 1977 and they were born in 1975. We have no trauma from our histories.

Up until recently, history has always been a story of trauma. After World War II, they needed to find a new identity for Japan. "We lost and we need to find ourselves." That's a sort of trauma. Kenzo Tange, Isozaki, Toyo, Shinohara, they all tried to do that. And in the 1970s, they approached history by calling it postmodernism. But after the failure of postmodernism, architects never discussed history because they were afraid to fail again.

For architects like Sejima, it is about the future for her. She never mentions history, but I would say her practice is really related to the traditions and history of Japan. Maybe Atelier Bow-Wow is a kind of turning point. From the beginning, they have mentioned history, and because I learned from them, I have been influenced. Our generation doesn't think of history as an enemy. Even now,

Go Hasegawa

Toyo Ito says "modernism is the enemy. We need to overcome it." I understand his position, but I don't think we need to deny modernism at all.

PH: In your book *Go Hasegawa: Conversations with European Architects,* you used the interview format to discuss European architectural generations.

GH: I think in Europe everyone is more of an individual. I remember when I gave a lecture at ETH in Zurich. It was my first lecture in Europe. I started my introduction. "I was teaching, I was studying at Tokyo Tech, and my professor was . . .," and they were a bit surprised, because they don't say things like that. Of course, they don't deny their influences and background, but they think of themselves as individual architects. I'm a bit embarrassed about what I did, but I also understand that I am strongly influenced by this culture of a genealogy of architects in Japan.

Instead of horizontal layers, we are more conscious of our vertical relationships: for instance, my relationship with Tokyo Tech as a school, instead of the horizontal connections between other architects of my generation.

PH: This is interesting, understanding architectural generations in plan or section.

GH: Yes, there are two ways of understanding history. The first is a vertical approach, which is very specific to Japan. But at the same time, we can find this horizontal approach all over the world. This matrix of approaches is my sense of history now.

PH: So, you had to leave Japan to see it?

GH: Yes. Maybe it's the same for everybody, but it's very difficult to be objective within this context. In Japan, I just live in Japan. My experience of teaching in Mendrisio, in Switzerland, was important for me. Because I had never studied or worked abroad, it was my first experience of seeing Japan from the outside.

PH: And why did you choose the interview format for your book?

GH: As a format it is an interview, but for me it was a kind of conversation. For example, Valerio Olgiati talked about his father, and that was very special. And a lot of Swiss architects were surprised in reading my book—"Oh, he talked about his father a lot!"—because he could open up to a Japanese architect.

That was my strategy. I behaved innocently: I noticed but pretended not to notice that he didn't want to be asked about his father, for example, so we're conscious about this kind of strategically innocent conversation.

PH: In fact, we may be having a strategically innocent conversation now. [Laughter]

GH: Yes!

Edited by Phu Hoang with Rachely Rotem

Second Nature:
Conversations in Tokyo

Phu Hoang with Rachely Rotem

Speaking across Generations
In the summer of 2018, Japan experienced several extreme weather events. Two record-breaking heat waves—of which one was the hottest in seventy-two years—brought heat index temperatures as high as 106°F in Tokyo.[1] Post-analysis of meteorological conditions indicated that the heat waves could never have happened without the impact of extreme climate change.[2] Along with the heat waves, there was also a 5.2-magnitude earthquake in Osaka, a typhoon in the Kansai region, and flash flooding in Hiroshima and Okayama prefectures. In this context of extreme weather and climate crisis, Phu Hoang and Rachely Rotem conducted research throughout the six climate zones of Japan, including a series of in-depth conversations with Japanese architects. Those architects—Go Hasegawa, Itsuko Hasegawa, Kengo Kuma, Fumihiko Maki, Ryue Nishizawa, and Takaharu and Yui Tezuka—represent five architectural generations, spanning over sixty years of Japanese architecture culture.

Each architect began their own practice during a period of social or environmental transformation in Japan, from Fumihiko Maki, a Metabolist architect who began designing for postwar Tokyo in the 1960s, to Itsuko Hasegawa, who embraced new technologies in the 1980s. They were followed by Kengo Kuma, who launched his practice during the economic crisis of the early 1990s, to Ryue Nishizawa and Takaharu and Yui Tezuka, who emerged at the end of this "lost decade," and Go Hasegawa, who gained international recognition after the Great East Japan Earthquake in 2011. Hoang and Rotem's conversations with these architects, spanning across generations, highlight common values that intersect architecture with the environment and with Japanese society.

Second Nature as Guide
MODU's definition of **second nature** served as a thread guiding these conversations. Second nature has two meanings. The first refers to the everyday habits so deeply ingrained in our spatial memory that they seem automatic: opening a window on a hot summer day or using an umbrella in the rain. When these habits form patterns of behavior in

society, they define the daily social relations of people interacting in their built and natural environments. The everyday act of crossing busy streets diagonally in Tokyo is different than the perpendicular crossings in New York City, as it involves different spatial habits. Unlearning environmental behaviors is the first step to living differently, as **social particles** adapting to the climate crisis.

Another meaning of second nature questions the commonly held belief that the environment is architecture's externality. This ideology has reinforced environmental borders, especially in Western architectural discourse, between the interior and the urban or the built and the natural. Second-nature thinking does not assume that architecture and the environment are distinct from each other. It sees them not in opposition, but instead as part of a continuum. The dual interpretations of second nature embed social behavior—and the unlearning of spatial habits—within architecture that is synchronous with the environment.

The idea of second nature raises an inevitable question: If second nature asks us to reimagine relationships between architecture and the environment, then what is first nature? First nature is based on the ideal of a pristine nature, one undisturbed by humans. This form of nature could only have existed prior to human settlements. Since there are few places on earth that have no trace of human intervention, first nature imagines an impossible scenario. In this way, it is an ideology representative of the kind of anthropocentric thinking that reinforces human exceptionalism.[3]

Above top: Meiji Jingu Gaien Park, Tokyo; built and natural environments structure each other

Above bottom: Omicho Market, Kanazawa; ice blocks at entrance provide passive cooling with social interaction

As tempting as the notion of a return to undisturbed nature may be, that concept of "return" only serves to further separate our built and natural environments. If the environment is the sum of the atmospheric phenomena that occur in a given place (regardless of human impact), it can be found in interior, exterior, or in-between spaces. It exists in urban, suburban, or rural settings. Second nature is, perhaps, a state in which there is no longer the desire to return to a nonexistent first nature. Our full attention can be focused on maintaining the environment we have, rather than seeking one that does not exist.

Hoang and Rotem discussed three central aspects of second nature with the architects: the mutable borders between interior and exterior, the extremely different scales of microarchitecture and mega-urbanism, and the inherently incomplete nature of architecture. Conversations about where architecture's borders are drawn evoked the Japanese tradition of architecture without walls, in which roofs and floors delimit spaces. This led to discussions of extremely differentiated scales. The countless microscale building "kernels" that comprise the most populated metropolis in the world create this extreme scale difference. Finally, the conversations turned to the incomplete and open-ended character of architecture, and its influence on both design process and built form. In their discussions, it became apparent that these Japanese architects have been working across generations on shared values, manifesting them differently in Japan's diverse climate regions. A continuous history of these five architectural generations reveals the shared intersecting themes of the environment, scale, and time.

Where the Inside Ends and Outside Begins
Where does the inside end and the outside begin? These architects believe that there are no borders—in other words, no separation between indoors and outdoors. Fumihiko Maki raised his own term, "open linkage," which is both a space and a larger system. He discussed historical linkages that produce diversity and unity, such as the open-air stoops in Amsterdam or the covered arcades of Bologna.[4] Maki's concept of group form—one of three collective forms that includes mega-form and compositional form—includes open linkages, which are typically an environmental threshold.[5]

In Maki's Hillside Terrace in Tokyo, the open linkages take the form of shaded voids between buildings over time. The project was built in six phases over a period of twenty-five years, resulting in a series of smaller buildings.[6] The linkages that emerged have distinct microclimates that vary from exterior to semi-exterior to semi-interior and interior. On a hot, humid summer day, it is more comfortable to walk through Hillside Terrace by avoiding the overheated street, traversing from one shaded linkage to another. It is at these environmental thresholds that Maki, in his writings, describes designing the space of a tree and its shade.[7]

In Ryue Nishizawa's Moriyama House, the house is reconceived as a group of independent structures. Each room of a traditional Japanese house is separated from the others and distributed around a site. The result is a complete reimagination of domestic and public life. To move from bedroom to living room requires leaving one structure, walking a short distance semi-outdoors, and entering another one. This involves unlearning—and relearning—spatial habits associated with interior domestic life. Every day, the owner, Moriyama-san, spends time that is not entirely indoors or outdoors, but in between the two in an **outdoor interior**. Nishizawa's design demonstrated a common Japanese quality that he observed, describing it as going from inside to outside gradually.[8]

Moriyama House mobilizes circulation as the threshold in between interior and exterior. It can be argued that the project is a commentary on Maki's group form. Atelier Bow-Wow's Yoshiharu Tsukamoto provided

the historical development of when he described the narrow gaps between Tokyo's buildings as "void metabolism."[9] Reconceiving the environmental borders of the house depends on simultaneously enlarging gaps—or open linkages—and reducing the scale of the structures. Moriyama House magnifies an existing condition common to many of Tokyo's residential neighborhoods: that of extreme scale difference between small houses and large urban neighborhoods. The house is not experienced differently than its surroundings because it is similarly a group of small structures separated by narrow gaps. In fact, Moriyama-san has taken to leaving a sign at the edge of his property indicating where the street ends and his house begins, in an effort to keep people from wandering into his home.

Above top: Moriyama House, Tokyo; sign at sidewalk asks visitors not to enter the house's outdoor circulation

Above bottom: Moriyama House, Tokyo; plantings and objects are used to block access

The traditional Japanese house is an architectural type deeply embedded in its architecture culture, embodying a culture's domestic rituals through its daily habits. Itsuko Hasegawa spent years researching traditional houses, and likens their typology to mushrooms in nature, spreading around the country with the wind. The six climate zones of Japan combine with a cultural history that catalogued twenty-four seasons attuned to harvest cycles. This has produced diverse house types that respond to climate and culture, reinventing building elements along the way. Hasegawa described the large roofs of houses in northern Aomori as responding to the region's heavy snows. The tall homes in Hida Takayama, a central region known for growing silkworms, have three stories so that silkworms can unravel their strands of fiber from the roofs. Traditional building elements such as the *engawa*, which literally means "edge side," are appropriate for hot climates since the wooden floor allows air to pass through for cooling.[10] Forming a perimeter around the rooms of a house, it provides access from inside to outside and serves as both circulation and threshold.

Both Maki and Nishizawa similarly mobilize circulation—not with the *engawa*, but with the ground as threshold. Moriyama House engages the ground with narrow exterior gaps between walls that allow for daily movements from inside to outside; in fact, the project can be understood as having its roots in Japanese farms, with daily movements between various small structures in the landscape. Hillside Terrace uses open linkages in the ground between buildings. Both projects demonstrate the first argument of second nature, connecting patterns of daily behavior with the experience of being in between the indoor and outdoor. Architecture does not need to reinforce separation; instead, it makes less distinction between architecture and the environment. Itsuko Hasegawa referred to this as "another nature" or, similarly, "second nature."[11]

Small Vastness
As the Moriyama house shows in miniature, with its ambiguities about where the city ends and the house begins, second nature is also based in the extreme differentiation of scales. The design of microscale buildings and interiors, when multiplied many times, defines the vast urban scale. Simultaneously considering both small and very large, or **small vastness**, is essential to reconceiving the relationship between interior and urban scales. The discussions with the Japanese architects were about Tokyo as a city of extreme scale difference. They did not see any contradictions within this condition, finding it a Western perspective that assigns discrete, or incremental, scales to architecture, the city, and the environment.

In Kengo Kuma's essay *Anti-Object*, he writes of being "sensitive to the size of pixels in the city. . . . [T]here are many layers of pixels." In conversation, Kuma imagined an ideal city of particles, or pixels, and described how it had become integral to his design methodology.[12] In the Bato Hiroshige Museum of Art in Tochigi, his design process began with the scale of a pixel that he would use for many parts of the building.

There, the wood louver is repeated as ceilings, roofs, and walls. The louver is an architectural detail at a small scale, but when multiplied many times it becomes an urban screen.[13] Layering small-scale pixels repeatedly allows Kuma to work at two scales at once, as well as working with both shadow and "rainbow." He described the rainbow as changing one's perspective as one moves through the space.[14]

These extremely different scales have references in traditional Japanese architecture. Among numerous examples, perhaps the most important is Katsura Imperial Villa, or the Katsura Detached Palace. Located in the western suburbs of Kyoto, it is an imperial residence with an expansive garden surrounding numerous small buildings. The current version began renovations in 1641 and can described as the **weather rooms** of a traditional palace, detached from each other and reconnected through a garden.[15] Thus, Katsura Detached Palace is its more appropriate name.

With its multiple thatched roof buildings, the palace also derives from the vernacular farmhouse of the Muromachi period (1336–1773). In his essay about Katsura, architect Kenzo Tange describes the farmhouses and their tea ceremonies as essential to a Japanese cultural belief in simplicity.[16] Teahouses, of which four can be found in the Katsura Detached Palace, are minimalist structures that embody the social behaviors of Zen Buddhism. The small teahouses demonstrate the interrelationship between small and large scales through the sublime weaving of architecture and landscape.

Above top: Katsura Detached Palace, Kyoto; traditional thatched roof on gatehouse structure

Above bottom: Mount Togakushi, Nagano; simple farm structure with layered roof construction

The relationship of scales has also been important to the work of Go Hasegawa, especially in his early house projects. In the Japanese language, there are nine different words that translate to "small." *Chiisai* is an adjective often used to describe small things in a complimentary way. As an example, the design of human-scaled spaces fosters social connections that are difficult to achieve with larger spaces. Go Hasegawa clarified that he seeks a more direct human scale, connected to individuals, and not the universal human scale he associates with Western architectural thinking. His projects combine very low ceilings with high ones, creating the experience of dynamically changing scales in a house. In his House in Kyodo, the low ceiling of the ground floor opens up to a high, vaulted upper floor for the clients, two editors with lots of books.[17]

Go Hasegawa argued that Tokyo's unique character of extremely different scales is possible because of the Japanese belief in a shared ground. A two-story house in Tokyo's Shinjuku neighborhood is experienced in a similar way as the tall tower next to it. Since they share a ground, their differences in size and height are relative. The ground equalizes differences so that the house and tower are seen individually and collectively. He described this as an "unconscious similarity."[18]

Second nature also argues for an interrelatedness of extremely different scales. This requires unlearning incremental thinking about scale, with architecture understood as one or two scales away from itself. This has served to separate architecture from the city and the environment. It is essential to understand how the small scale of daily habits and behavior influences extremely large urban scales. Designing simultaneously for two extreme limits of scale—architectural and climate—is necessary to understand how our daily behaviors impact the climate crisis.

Architecture's Incomplete Nature
Another theme that emerged in these conversations was the inherently incomplete nature of architecture. In our societies of change, marked by extreme climate and social disruption, when is architecture ever truly "complete"? This question is especially relevant in Tokyo, a city always in a state of reconstructing itself—an **incomplete whole**. As Maki pointed out, when a building in Japan no longer suits its use, it is demolished and a new purpose-built one is erected.[19] This occurs constantly throughout its cities, producing the effect of a city in a continuous state of incompletion.

Along with Katsura Detached Palace, the Ise Shrine is one of Japan's most important works of architecture. Kenzo Tange considers it to be the "starting point of the Japanese architectural tradition."[20] The holiest shrine of the Shinto religion, it has an Inner Precinct that is dismantled and rebuilt every twenty years. It uses the exact dimensions of the "original," and has been rebuilt sixty-two times over 2,000 years.[21] This process of unbuilding and rebuilding recalls the Japanese phrase "mono no aware," which translates to the impermanence, or ephemerality, of things. It can be argued that the Ise Shrine is not only one of Japan's oldest wood structures, but also its longest-running incomplete project.

In discussions about architecture's incomplete nature, Itsuko Hasegawa understood that her projects are not completed for years after construction is finished. She explained that only when a project was used as a community envisioned it would it be complete. During her design process, she organizes community feedback sessions to understand how a community plans to use their future architecture. Itsuko Hasegawa's first public building, Shonandai Cultural Center, was not "completed" for ten years. After construction, she programmed a series of community workshops, including with local children, to teach them about architecture and facilitate using the building as originally envisioned.[22]

Above top: Midtown garden, Tokyo; stone pavers in park

Above bottom: Ryoan-ji, Kyoto; Zen rock garden

Takaharu and Yui Tezuka argued for an even longer timeline of architectural completion. They contended that the end of construction is only the beginning. Yui Tezuka posited that architecture is empty until it is occupied by people—it is only then that architecture has started. Her partner, Takaharu, continued that architecture can only be completed when it is demolished; it remains incomplete so that people can continue to adapt it for their own use. Tezuka Architects has built over 180 projects, though none have yet been dismantled. By their own estimation, their practice has not completed any projects at all.[23]

These conversations about architectural incompletion highlight a particularly Japanese perspective on the slow passage of time. A building remains incomplete beyond the needs of its occupants. Architecture's inherent incompleteness frames their ideas about historical time, which is not based on fixed time periods but is open-ended and continuous. Each of the Japanese architects are deeply aware of the continual development of ideas in projects that preceded their own. It has already been pointed out that Maki's Hillside Terrace and Nishizawa's Moriyama House exist within this open history. It can also be argued that contemporary Japanese architects are in a long dialogue with their historical precedents—Nishizawa argued that his work was very traditional and wondered if he had done anything new.[24] From the traditional house type to Katsura Detached Palace to the

Ise Shrine, open-ended histories continue to provide new ground for contemporary projects.

Second-Nature Architecture
Second nature envisions architecture and the environment as extensions of each other. It is not a binary condition of being indoors or outdoors but one of atmospheric thresholds where both environments can be experienced. The built environment can be designed to be more proactive in supporting, or even strengthening, the natural environment.

We can unlearn our habits of controlling the environment to learn new habits that are not overly dependent on carbon-emitting fossil fuel sources. The experience of being outdoors while connected to the indoors is possible with microclimatic design. Conversely, design strategies of being indoors with the benefits of the outdoors would include low-energy, mixed-mode systems. Collectively learning a new spatial habit of being in between environments— both the city in the room and the room in the city— can prompt necessary changes to social behaviors. These changes would serve to support a drastically changing climate.

Above top: The Hakone Open-Air Museum, Hakone; hot spring foot bath outside of museum

Above bottom: Minami-Ikebukuro Park, Tokyo; large children's slide built into a hill

The numerous extreme weather events in Japan during the summer of 2018 made the need for action apparent, in Japan and elsewhere. Architects, as cultural practitioners, must understand the climate crisis not simply as an environmental project; it is also an urgent social and cultural project. In the case of the Japanese architects in these conversations, it requires relearning—or not forgetting—the spatial habits that have existed culturally before, whether in a previous generation or centuries earlier. It means designing architecture in between indoors and outdoors, small and large scales, the built and the incomplete. These ideas embodied in Japanese architectural thinking can be instrumental to other cultures, prompting a reconception of architecture and the environment as existing on the same spectrum: both/and rather than either/or.

Second-nature architecture prompts us to rethink our environmental habits, which prompts changes to how we live in our near and distant futures. This is the dual meaning of second nature—changing daily behaviors to live better in the age of extreme climate change.

1. Walter Sim, "Earthquakes, Rains, Heatwave, Typhoon: Japan's Brutal Summer of 2018," *The Straits Times*, September 10, 2018.

2. Yukiko Imada et al., "The July 2018 High Temperature Event in Japan Could Not Have Happened without Human-Induced Global Warming," SOLA, Meteorological Society of Japan, May 22, 2019, p. 1.

3. Steven Vogel, *Thinking Like a Mall: Environmental Philosophy after the End of Nature* (Cambridge, MA, 2016), p. 25.

4. Fumihiko Maki and Jerry Goldberg, "Linkage in Collective Form," *Ekistics* 14, no. 82 (Athens, 1962): 101.

5. Fumihiko Maki, "Investigations in Collective Form," School of Architecture, Washington University, special publication no. 2 (1964), p. 5.

6. Ibid., p. 167.

7. Ibid., p. 184.

8. Yoshiharu Tsukamoto, "Escaping the Spiral of Intolerance: Fourth Generation Houses and Void Metabolism," in *Tokyo Metabolizing* (Tokyo, 2010), p. 29.

9. Ibid., p. 172.

10. Itsuko Hasegawa, *Miniseries 5: Architecture as Another Nature* (New York, 1991).

11. Ibid., p. 177.

12. Kengo Kuma, *Architecture Words 2: Anti-Object* (London, 2013).

13. Ibid., p. 178.

14. Ibid., p. 179.

15. Kenzo Tange, *Katsura: Tradition and Creation in Japanese Architecture* (New Haven, CT, 1960), p. 14.

16. Ibid., p. 192.

17. Ibid., p. 193.

18. Ibid., p. 169.

19. Kenzo Tange, *Katsura* p. 27.

20. Kenzo Tange, *Ise: Prototype of Japanese Architecture* (Cambridge, MA, 1965), p. 18.

21. Ibid., p. 56.

22. Ibid., p. 175.

23. Ibid., p. 189.

24. Ibid., p. 184.

Koishikawa Botanical Garden, Tokyo

Forward:
Indoor Urbanism

Architecture and the city have often been understood through oppositions—as building versus urbanism, object versus surroundings, and interior versus exterior. Indoor urbanism does not focus on establishing differences, but instead intersects architecture and cities with the environment. Since both are inextricable from the air, ground, and water that surrounds them, the "environment" is understood as being both outdoors and indoors. Indoor urbanism recognizes that architecture and cities are situated on an environmental continuum, as a matter of degrees rather than absolutes.

Indoor urbanism's character takes several forms: as gradations between the indoor and the outdoor, the open and the enclosed, and even the artificial and the living. Degrees of each character overlap with another, erasing oppositions while providing experiences of being in between one and the other. This can mean being indoors while having some of the experiences of being outdoors. If city parks are understood as artificial landscapes that mimic nature, can architecture do the same with its interiors? Urban spaces might include interior atmospheres. In other words, being inside-out or outside-in, suggesting an open exchange between architecture, cities, and the environment. Here, the environment is understood as everything—either living or nonliving— that influences organisms.

Though differentiated by just one term—"indoor" instead of "interior"— the definition of indoor urbanism is entirely different from the more commonly used "interior urbanism." Interior urbanism refers to interior spaces, large in scale and typically separated by glass, that are abstractions of urban character.[1] Following Reyner Banham, who argued for interiors to be reconceived as artificial environments,[2] late modernism had numerous examples of interior urbanism—for example, Buckminster's Fuller's utopian vision of the "Dome over Manhattan." On the other hand, Archizoom's No-Stop City[3] is social critique in the form of dystopian imagery. While diverse, these urban imaginaries all influenced their built realities, from John Portman's hotel lobbies to countless international airport terminals. Theoretical and built works alike reinforce modernism's borders between architecture and the environment. Interior urbanism relies on environmental separation for its volumes of mechanically conditioned air.[4] Indoor urbanism, on the other hand, argues for less separation with more atmospheric exchange. The bidirectional flow of inside-out and outside-in can result in an architecture with fewer boundaries—both environmental and social.

Indoor urbanism's "outside-in" form brings exterior atmospheres into building interiors. Everyday examples include sunrooms and open-air interiors. Conversely, "inside-out" brings indoor activities to outdoor spaces, from open-air museums to outdoor schools. While these examples are increasingly common, they also prompt speculative climate futures. As the climate crisis intensifies, it is necessary for architecture and cities to reduce their reliance on fully climatized interiors and the carbon-based fuels that make them. There is an increasing need for inventive low-energy architecture. This need does not have to subscribe to an idea that designing with the environment is not as original as other design methods. On the contrary, the linked crises of environmental and social justice require the design disciplines' most conceptual and advanced thinking—now even more essential given our realities.

Three concepts define indoor urbanism: **public floor**, **incomplete whole**, and **second nature**. They form a framework for designing with microclimates that produce thermal diversity as both matter and atmosphere. The public floor calls the divisions separating public and private into question while elevating everyday interactions between indoor and outdoor realms. The incomplete whole connects the unenclosed with the incomplete, from a spatial to a time-based understanding of architecture and the city. Finally, second nature has a dual meaning, alluding to spatial habits that become behaviors and hybridizing architecture with the environment. All three concepts assume an interdependence between the environmental atmosphere and social behavior, which benefits both individuals and communities.

Atmospheres create the sensory experiences that inform daily acts, which in turn become spatial habits. This can occur while walking on the sidewalks of New York, within the incomplete structures of Rome, or living in Tokyo's micro-buildings. Environmental cognition, which engages human senses beyond the visual, connects people to their surroundings through heat, sound, and smell. It especially occurs through thermosensation—the sense that allows the body to perceive heat and cold. The somatosensory system contains heat sensors in the skin that detect thermal changes. Studies indicate that exposure to cooler and warmer temperatures—a change from constant conditions—can improve physical health. Specifically, these changes improve the body's metabolism while reducing metabolic diseases like obesity and diabetes.

Over 80 percent of our time is spent indoors, with much of it under the regime of constant temperature.[5] Redefining indoor comfort reveals the limitations of the American Standard of Heating, Refrigerating, and Air-Conditioning Engineers' (ASHRAE) standard of thermal comfort. Increasing both the temperature range and time spent with thermal diversity can change perceptions toward microclimates. Mixed-mode heating, ventilation, and air conditioning (HVAC) systems already incorporate natural ventilation to reduce energy use. Thinking beyond mechanical systems, what are the strategies for low-energy architecture that better incorporates natural phenomena?

Designing with thermal buffers—the space in between indoors and outdoors—minimizes heating and cooling loads because it reduces climatization. Reconsidering the ASHRAE comfort zone, it is important to passively mitigate hot or cold air before it enters a building. Thermal buffers alleviate differences between interiors and exteriors, which can significantly reduce energy use. One scenario reimagines building courtyards by converting them into tree-filled greenhouses. These greenhouses would maintain an energy-saving microclimate year-round, warmed in the winter by closing an operable roof and cooled in the summer by opening it (along with the trees' cool microclimate). Atmospheric phenomena, combined with active technologies, create architectural experiences from these thermal buffers. The buffers, with their temperature variability, improve physical health while reducing energy and carbon impact.

Considering technology beyond architecture's borders, today's cities are vast networks of invisible data. Though it is often misused for profit or surveillance, such data is nonetheless necessary for improving environmental and social accessibility. It can be used to identify social inequities, and this information sharpens communities' ability to improve inclusivity. Sensing and simulation technologies—from thermal imaging to geographic information systems (GIS)—render the unseen visible, revealing the distribution of both natural and man-made resources for healthy environments. In New York City, the NYC Open Data website provides open-source information from air quality to sidewalk access to tree canopy coverage.[5] Citizen data scientists provide their software to the public, ranging from mapping the accessible sidewalk widths throughout New York to an immersive 3-D model of the city that can show a new building in relation to its surroundings.[6] Civic-minded organizations can use this knowledge to better understand the inequities faced by residents—especially those in marginalized communities—and it can help them underscore the need for more equitable access. This technology can foster civic participation rather than disengagement with their city's **public floor**.

Encouraging citizens to participate in their social infrastructure can promote a sense of ownership. Though seemingly minor, daily acts that occur repeatedly—from reading on a park bench to eating lunch in a plaza—increase commitment to the commons. This includes parks and plazas, but also small, overlooked resources. City sidewalks and their micro-urban structures—benches, bus stops, and kiosks—allow people to participate in urban microclimates. Private property also has assets, especially immaterial resources like the cooler air of building canopies and trees. The New York Public Library launched an outdoor reading room program based on the Department of Transportation's requirements for outdoor dining sheds during the COVID-19 pandemic.[7] These public seating sheds improved outdoor comfort while bringing the library outside as a community facility. Increasing the quality of, and access to, shared resources, whether public or private, is often a design question. For example, can building envelopes include small areas for people to rest in shade before continuing their daily routine?

What are other urban futures that prompt environmental participation? Perhaps a new kind of all-season room can let in rain and snow as well as sun? Instead of being isolated from any precipitation, the room can be designed as semi-exterior—complete with weatherproof materials and floor drains. People have sheltered experiences with summer rains and winter snowfalls in a room that serves as a thermal buffer for the interiors. These experiences can transform environmental perceptions, allowing us to rethink the environmental role of microclimatic spaces. This gives physical form to the idea of **second nature**—especially the design of architecture and cities that support the environment.

Designing for participatory action is not without its risks. Often, community board meetings privilege those with more free time, or jobs that allow for more flexible schedules. Businesses and individuals with more financial resources have more voice in urban planning processes.

Citizen-based participation with the environment does not necessarily solve this intractable issue, but if cities and building owners provided better microclimatic infrastructure, it would be a step forward. Inviting people to use these shared resources involves spending less time in fully interior spaces separated from the outdoors, while promoting ownership through daily interactions.

Designing for environmental and social participation involves a different approach. Fixed, singular design outcomes are not sufficient with the variability of climate and the changing needs of people. To adapt to these changes, designers can speculate on the multiple possible, in addition to probable, futures. In our societies of continual change, a building often outlasts its intended program, raising questions about how we define architectural completion. Given the changing climate, programs, and even sites, when is architecture ever "complete"? Through the carbon-reducing benefit of adaptive reuse, parking decks have been converted into schools and churches into housing. Whether the future of a stadium involves sports events or opera performances— or both at different times—involves the voice of its community. The idea of the **incomplete whole** requires the participation of many to make it "whole."

Understanding architecture and cities as constantly changing provokes questions about the rationality of singular, fixed programs. Since no future program can be predicted, how can architectural adaptability be part of a design method? Perhaps including dynamic atmospheres within architectural programs is a framework for adaptability. Typically, programs are defined by human or technological activity—for example, a library or a data center. Intersecting programs with atmospheres, either a place or a state, introduces multiple futures. Possible programs might include a library, a kindergarten, housing, and an office. Atmospheres can be a garden, a forest, a canyon, or simply open-air. Combinations can vary, since designing an "open-air library" is different than designing a "forest library." These programmatic atmospheres connect interior programs with dynamic exterior environments, resulting in a more open definition of architectural program.

An open-air library can include areas open to the city yet still be sheltered from the elements. These areas use multimedia content not easily damaged by exposure. The library enables experiences, like reading outdoors, using architectural elements designed to reduce temperature extremes and sun exposure. The open border of this library involves technology; eliminating the book checkout desk allows members of the public to freely read indoors, outdoors, or in between. Alternatively, a forest library could be a retreat. Sheltered in a forest and surrounded by trees, it is micro-scaled and designed for quiet study. It can bring the outdoors in, with materials typically used for exteriors. An indoor tree in the reading area can make use of sensors that provide updates on the tree's health and monitor its microclimate. Whether environmentally inside-out—like the open-air library—or outside-in—like the forest library—both spaces harness the conceptual framework of indoor urbanism.

The essential argument of indoor urbanism advocates for a heightened observation of architecture and the city—which prompts the intersection of both with the environment. It recasts the threshold where the inside ends and the outside begins, envisioning it as an expanded thermal buffer occupied by people and filled with atmospheric qualities. The crisis of climate change is not simply an environmental project; it is also a social project, one that requires all the cultural resources of allied design disciplines. Indoor urbanism seeks to redefine the spatial habits that are essential with extreme climate change. From the urgency of our environmental realities and their social impact emerges a synthesis of architecture, city, and environment.

1. Charles Rice, *Interior Urbanism: Architecture, John Portman, and Downtown America* (London, 2016).

2. Reyner Banham, *The Architecture of the Well-Tempered Environment* (Chicago, 1984).

3. Andrea Branzi, *No-Stop City* (Orléans, 2006).

4. David Gissen, *Manhattan Atmospheres: Architecture, the Interior Environment, and Urban Crisis* (Minneapolis, 2014).

5. Open Data for All New Yorkers, retrieved from https://opendata.cityofnewyork.us/.

6. Welcome to the NYC Open Data Project Gallery, retrieved from https://opendata.cityofnewyork.us/projects/.

7. Karrie Jacobs, "Why Libraries May Never Stop Being People Places," *The New York Times*, August 21, 2022.

Credits

Mapping: Horizontal City

Phu Hoang, Rachely Rotem, Alice Fang, Ilse de Sutter, Diego Fernandez Morales, Jiri Vala, Tom Sterling, Brenda Lim

Episode: Invisible Atmospheres

Rachely Rotem, Phu Hoang, Kamilla Csegzi Jonathan Izen

Cloud Seeding, Holon

Rachely Rotem, Phu Hoang, Kamilla Csegzi

Geotectura (collaborator), Avihay Shoval, Ho-Yan Cheung (structural), Aviad Bar Ness (photography), Ori Zifroni (videography)

Sponsors: Alubin, Palram

Intake

Phu Hoang, Rachely Rotem, Chih-Ying Wong, Munyoung Lee, Margaux Young

Isoenv (environmental)

Outdoor Room

Phu Hoang, Rachely Rotem, Amanda Morgan, Xinran Ma, Yuri Jeong, Hugo Santibanez, Demar Jones, Emanuel Admassu, Chad Murphy

Arup, Beijing Institute of Architectural Design (structural), Matthew Niederhauser (photography)

Episode: Weather Uncontrol

Phu Hoang, Rachely Rotem, Kamilla Csegzi, Sara Dionis Sevilla, Chad Murphy, Evan Collins

Amanda Parkes (engineering), Zack Freedman (fabrication), Brett Beyer (photography)

Sponsors: New York State Council on the Arts, Rauschenberg Foundation

Heart Squared

Rachely Rotem, Phu Hoang, Jiri Vala, Ilse De Sutter, Tom Sterling, Brenda Lim

Eric Forman (collaborator), Silman (structural), New Project (fabrication), Frank Oudeman / OTTO (photography), Times Square Arts and Afterimaging (videography)

Sponsors: The Andy Warhol Foundation for the Arts, The National Endowment for the Arts, New York City Department of Cultural Affairs in partnership with the City Council, The Ripple Foundation, Silman, and New Project

Episode: Field

Phu Hoang, Rachely Rotem, Michael McDowell, Zhenwei Zhong, Kelly Yuen

Second Life

Rachely Rotem, Phu Hoang, Jiri Vala, Tom Sterling, Zhenwei Zhong, Shu Du

Credits: Silman (structural), Transsolar (environmental)

Episode: Platform

Rachely Rotem, Phu Hoang, Daniele Bobbio, Shu Du, Margarida Osorio

Transsolar (environmental), Kristi Cheramie (landscape)

Mapping: Urban Voids

Rachely Rotem, Phu Hoang, Jiri Vala

Recording: Incomplete City

Rachely Rotem, Phu Hoang

Episode: Disappearing Ruins

Phu Hoang, Rachely Rotem

Episode: Flexing Structures

Phu Hoang, Rachely Rotem, Kamilla Csegzi

Mini Tower One

Phu Hoang, Rachely Rotem, Diego Fernandez Morales, Tom Sterling, Alice Fang, Jiri Vala

Silman (structural), Engineering Solutions (MEP), Zero Energy Design (envelope), Transsolar (environmental)

Episode: Psychometric Thresholds

Rachely Rotem, Phu Hoang, Diego Fernandez Morales

Mapping: Mini Towers

Phu Hoang, Rachely Rotem, Adeline Chum

Promenade

Phu Hoang, Rachely Rotem, Tom Sterling, Brenda Lim

Identity Architects (architect of record), Kudela & Weinheimer (landscape), CJG Engineers (structural), ASEI Engineering (MEP), ALJ Lindsey (civil)

Double House

Rachely Rotem, Phu Hoang, Diego Fernandez Morales

Exhale

Phu Hoang, Rachely Rotem, Ammr Vandal, Federica von Euw, Sunghyun Park

Arup, YH Engineering (structural), Miami-Dade Environmental Resource Management (artificial reef program), Robin Hill (photography)

Habits and Habitats

Rachely Rotem, Phu Hoang, Diego Fernandez Morales

Cairn Landscape Architects (landscape), Silman (structural), Transsolar (environmental), Energy 1 (MEP), Nelson Engineering (geotechnical), Valley West Engineering (civil) Water Design (pool design), Lisa Jean Moore (sociology)

Conversations in Tokyo

Phu Hoang, Rachely Rotem

Fumihiko Maki, Maki and Associates, Itsuko Hasegawa, Itsuko Hasegawa Atelier, Kengo Kuma, Kengo Kuma and Associates, Ryue Nishizawa, Office of Ryue Nishizawa, Takaharu and Yui Tezuka (Tezuka Architects), Go Hasegawa (Go Hasegawa and Associates), Kenji Seo (translation)

MODU
Field Guide to Indoor Urbanism

Editors: Phu Hoang, Rachely Rotem

Project management: Adam Jackman

Copyediting: Aaron Bogart

Translations: Kenji Seo
(Conversations in Tokyo)

Graphic design: MGMT. design

Typeface: Favorit

Production: Thomas Lemaître

Reproductions: Schwabenrepro GmbH,
Fellbach

Printing: Livonia Print, Riga

Paper: Munken Polar, 150 g/m^2

Published by
Hatje Cantz Verlag GmbH
Mommsenstraße 27
10629 Berlin
www.hatjecantz.com
A Ganske Publishing Group Company

ISBN 978-3-7757-5118-6

Printed in Latvia

Cover illustration: MODU

The Architectural League of New York
served as fiscal sponsor for the New York
State Council on the Arts support

Knowlton —— School